T0340033

Chinese Research Perspectives on Population and Labor, Volume 8

Chinese Research Perspectives on Population and Labor

International Series Advisors

Kam Wing Chan (*University of Washington*)
William Lavely (*University of Washington*)

VOLUME 8

The titles published in this series are listed at *brill.com/crpo*

Chinese Research Perspectives on Population and Labor, Volume 8

Towards High-quality Employment

Edited by

GAO Wenshu
CHENG Jie

Translated by ZHANG Xiaonan

Published with financial support of the Innovation Program of the Chinese Academy of Social Sciences.

Typeface for the Latin, Greek, and Cyrillic scripts: "Brill". See and download: brill.com/brill-typeface.

ISSN 2212-7518
ISBN 978-90-04-69325-8 (hardback)
ISBN 978-90-04-70778-8 (e-book)
DOI 10.1163/9789004707788

This book is printed on acid-free paper and produced in a sustainable manner.

Contents

Figures and Tables

Figures

Tables

CHAPTER 1

Labor Supply and Demand in China during the Fourteenth Five-Year Plan Period

Xiang Jing* and Cai Yifei**

1 Projections of China's Labor Supply and Demand during the Fourteenth FYP Period and in the Short and Medium Term

1.1 *Projections of Labor Supply during the Fourteenth FYP Period and in the Short and Medium Term*

Employment stability is one of the major objectives of economic development for socialist countries, and projections of the size and structure of labor supply are important bases for development of short- and medium-term employment policies. Labor supply can be measured in terms of the stock and the flow. The stock refers to the number of the economically active population, and the flow means the number of new entrants to the labor market. For calculation, the labor supply of the current year is the sum of the labor stock at the end of the previous year and the number of new entrants to the labor market in the current year, or, the labor flow in the current year. The flow demonstrates the increment and growth rate of labor supply, while the stock reflects the overall situation of the labor market. This section forecasts China's labor supply during the fourteenth FYP period and the following years based on the stock (total size) and flow (increment) of the labor force.

1.1.1 Projections of Working-Age Population

This research uses the model-based analytical framework of population migration proposed by Xiang et al.[1] and the cohort component method for projection of China's population from 2019 to 2050. The projections are based on the size of population by household registration in urban and rural areas, age

---

* Xiang Jing is an assistant professor at the Institute of Population and Labor Economics, CASS, and her research interests are population economics and employment.

** Cai Yifei is an associate professor at the Institute of Population and Labor Economics, CASS, and his research interests are regional economy and employment.

1 Xiang Jing, and Zhong Funing, "The Reestimation of China's Rural-to-Urban Migration and the Scale of Migration Population: An Analysis based on a Whole Village Survey," *Studies in Labor Economics* 5, 2(2017): 3–18.

group and gender, and the rural-to-urban migration rates by age group and gender. The hypotheses for the cohort component method are as follows:

a.   Fertility rate. It is agreed among researchers that China's total fertility rate (TFR) is 1.5 or so.[2] From 2000 to 2010, the TRF of permanent residents in China's urban areas ranged between 0.94 and 1.22, and while the figure was higher, 1.43 to 1.73, in rural areas.[3] Underreporting and omissions considered, China's TFR is 1.6. Couples in China are allowed to have a second child if the wife or husband is an only child starting from 2014. Some researchers believe that this policy will raise China's TFR to the replacement level of 2.2, which will change the country's demographic trajectory, and cause China's population to peak at 1.501 billion.[4] In this research, however, we believe that people's need for social participation increases in tandem with economic development, resulting in a change in fertility intentions towards an increasingly lower fertility rate. Relaxation of birth policies does not lead to significant changes in people's fertility decisions. Therefore, this research examines three TFRs at 2.1, 1.8 and 1.4 respectively corresponding to the high, medium and low level.

b.   Average life expectancy. Based on the mortality revealed in China's fifth national population census, some researchers estimate that the average life expectancy was 69.84 years for men and 73.40 years for women in 2000 in China.[5] *World Health Statistics 2018* issued by the World Health Organization (WHO) in 2018 shows that the average life expectancy in China was 76.4 years, and the figure was 75 years for men and 77.9 years for women. Considering the situation in China, it is presumed that between 2020 and 2050, the average life expectancy for men and women in China will continue to grow, though at a slower pace, so the average life expectancy will be seventy-seven years for men and eighty years for women by 2050.

Projections show that the working-age population in China and its share in the country's total population will continue to decline. During the fourteenth

---

2 Guo Zhigang, "On China's Fertility Rate in the 1990s," *Population Research* 28, 2(2004). Zhu Qin, "Estimation of China's Fertility Rate from 2000 to 2010: A Preliminary Study based on Data from the Sixth National Population Census," *Chinese Journal of Population Science*, 4(2012).

3 Hao Juan and Qiu Changrong, "A Comparative Analysis of Urban and Rural Fertility Rates in China since 2000," *South China Population* 26, 5(2011).

4 Zhai Zhenwu, Zhang Xianling, and Jin Yong'ai, "Demographic Consequences of an Immediate Transition to a Universal Two-child Policy," *Population Research*, 2(2014).

5 Chen Wei, "Projection of China's Population from 2005 to 2050," *Population Research*, 4(2006).

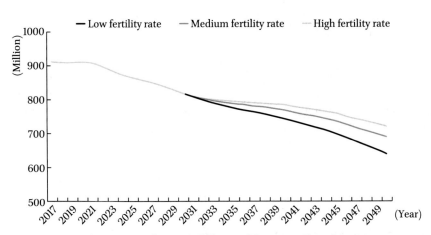

FIGURE 1.1   Working-age population aged fifteen to fifty-nine in China from 2017 to 2050

FYP period, the size of China's working-age population aged fifteen to fifty-nine will fall from about 910 million at the end of the thirteenth FYP period to 640–720 million in 2050 (see Figure 1.1). Consequently, the share of working-age population in China's total population will drop from 65.64 percent in 2018 to 53–54 percent in 2050. Relaxation of birth-control policies and a higher fertility rate lead to a significant increase in the total population, but there is a lag between the rise in fertility rate and the increase in labor supply. The projections of China's working-age population aged fifteen to fifty-nine from 2018 to 2031 based on three levels of fertility rate hardly show any difference. The different fertility rates mainly cause differences in projections of the total population.

Therefore, it will be at least fourteen years before the effect of China's new birth policies on slowing down the decline in labor supply can be felt.[6] From 2019 to 2031, the projections of working-age population based on three levels of fertility rates are the same, falling from 911 million from 2019 to 809 million in 2031. Starting from 2032, the projected declining rates of labor supply based on three levels of fertility rates become different. If China's TFR remains at the current level of 1.6, its total labor supply will drop from 803 million in 2032 to 690 million in 2050. If its TFR is raised to 2.1, close to the replacement

---

6   There is a time lag between the adjustment to fertility policies and the change in working-age population, because the change in fertility rate mainly has an immediate impact on the number of newborns, and newborns will not become a member of the working-age population until fifteen years later.

level, China's working-age population aged fifteen to fifty-nine will drop from 805 million in 2032 to 720 million in 2050.

1.1.2   Projections of the Number of New Entrants to the Labor Market

New entrants to the labor market refer to people of working age who have just entered the job market after completing a stage of education. Therefore, they are both labor and human capital. For estimation of the labor force with human capital, based on the size of the labor force and the enrollment rate and other information of different education stages, the composition of the labor force by educational attainment can be obtained. The number of new entrants to the labor market also rests with the labor force participation rate. Currently, there are two main estimation methods. One is to forecast the labor supply trends using nonparametric or time series models.[7] The other is to use a model in which the changing labor force participation rate is an influencing factor to forecast the labor force participation rate, which is then multiplied by the working-age population to calculate the labor supply. An important factor leading to the declining labor force participation rate is that people receive more years of education and start job hunting for the first time at an older age than before as a result of economic and social development.[8] Since the projections of labor force participation rate in many researches are based on the working-age population instead of the number of new entrants to the labor market, the existing methods for estimation of new labor force do not apply to this research. Therefore, unlike the existing analytical frameworks, this research forecasts the increase in China's labor force and human capital based on the share of the people leaving different stages of education and educational statistics.[9]

In China, compulsory education starts at the age of six. Since nine-year compulsory education became universally available to people aged six to fifteen in China in the 1980s, it has remained an important stage of education which prepares people for the labor market. After graduating from a junior secondary school, people can either further study at a senior secondary school or a vocational school, or enter the job market. Graduates from senior secondary schools can further study at a junior college or a university, or start job hunting.

7   Qi Guoyou, Zhou Aiping, and Zeng Saixing, "The Forecast on the Number of Surplus Labor Force in China Rural Areas in 2004–2020 and Some Countermeasures on Transferring Surplus Labor Force," *Journal of Northeast Agricultural University*, 5(2005).

8   Wang Jinying, and Lin Lili, "Analysis on Labor Force Participation Rate and Labor Supply in the Future in China," *Population Journal*, 4(2006).

9   Zhang Juwei, and Cai Yifei, "Forecasting China's Labor Supply and Demand and the Unemployment Structure in the 13th Five-Year Plan Period," *Population Research* 40, 1(2016): 38–56.

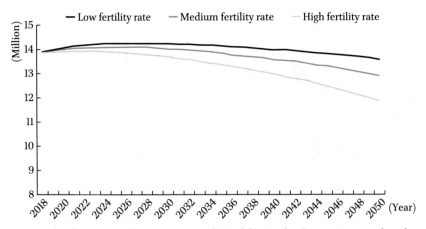

FIGURE 1.2   Projections of new entrants to China's labor market from 2018 to 2050 based on three levels of fertility rates

College graduates of working age can either continue to study or enter the job market. Apparently, newcomers to the labor market each year are primarily the people who have just left school and started job hunting. It is thus feasible to estimate the number of new entrants to the labor market according to the share of people leaving school in the working-age population. For calculation, the coefficients for the share of people leaving school are estimated according to the dropout rates of different education stages.

The above method is used for projection of the number of new entrants to China's labor market and their composition by educational attainment, the results of which are shown in Figure 1.2 and Figure 1.3. Overall the increase in labor force changes in tandem with that of the total population. The annual increase in China's labor force is expected to peak at 13.9 million to 14.11 million in 2026 and decline afterwards. Judging by the educational attainment, there will be a significant improvement in the human capital levels of the new entrants to China's labor market, the bulk of which will have at least completed junior college education. Estimation shows that the share of people with at least an associate degree in the new entrants to China's labor market will rise from 71.8 percent in 2018 to 73.4 percent in 2050. Such improvement in human capital levels is in line with China's rising enrollment rate of higher education following the expansion of master's programs.

The universal access to education and expansion of education at different levels inevitably lead to the improvement in human capital levels of the labor force. Job creation for new entrants to the labor market is vital to social stability. College graduates have been facing great challenges in job hunting in recent years. Projections of the annual increase in China's labor force show

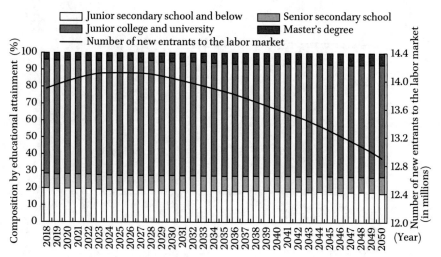

FIGURE 1.3   Number of new entrants to China's labor market from 2018 to 2050 and their
composition by educational attainment

that the number of new entrants to China's labor market with at least an associate degree will peak at about 10.12 million (from 2019 to 2037, there will be
more than ten million such newcomers to the labor market every year). Based
on the employment rate of 84.6 percent of college graduates in China, every
year, about 1.54 million college graduates have difficulties finding a job.[10] That
does not include graduates who choose to further study, start their own businesses or go to flexible employment. Considering that college graduates have
a high level of human capital, the failure to ensure jobs for them is not only a
waste of investment in education, but also demonstrates the absence of optimal resource allocation.

1.1.3   Projections of New Migrant Workers

Migrant workers are important members of the new entrants to China's urban
labor market. In 2018, migrant workers in China totaled 288 million, including
170 million working outside of the towns of registered household residence.
From the perspective of time series, the number of migrant workers in China
started declining in 2018. Statistics show that the increase in China's migrant
workers peaked at more than twelve million in 2010, and it has been declining afterwards, and recorded a negative growth in 2018. In 2018, the number
of migrant workers in China dropped by 520,000 from the previous year. As

---

10   Yue Changjun et al., "An Empirical Study on Graduates' Employment: Based on 2017
National Survey," *Journal of East China Normal University* (*Educational Sciences*), 5(2018).

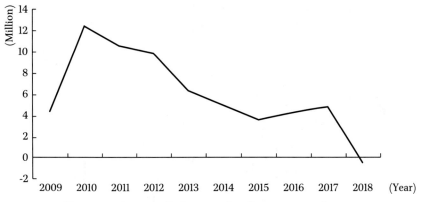

FIGURE 1.4   Year-on-year increase of migrant workers from 2009 to 2018

population ageing is accelerating and the working-age population is shrink-ing in China, a proper understanding of the trend in the number of migrant workers during the fourteenth FYP period is highly relevant to the develop-ment of the labor market and the economy. Growth curve modeling and time series analysis are mainly used for projection of the supply of migrant workers. Some researchers also forecast the increase in the number of migrant work-ers based on statistics by urban and rural areas.[11] Since migrant workers are rural-to-urban migrants of working age, a method similar to the one used in the above section is used for forecasting in this section. The supply of migrant workers is estimated based on ages and the rural-to-urban migration rate by age and gender.

The human capital levels of migrant workers have crucial impact on eco-nomic and social development. Therefore, for projection of the supply of migrant workers, in addition to forecasting the number, we also forecasted their human capital levels according to the share of new migrant workers leav-ing school at different stages of education in the total.

The supply of migrant workers in China from 2018 to 2050 is estimated based on the share of rural-to-urban migrants in the total population, and the human capital levels of migrant workers are estimated according to the share of people leaving school. The results are shown in Figure 1.5 and Figure 1.6. According to the *Migrant Workers Monitoring Survey Report 2018* issued by the NBS, the total number of migrant workers in China in 2018 was 286 million, down by 520,000 from the previous year. The projection of the total number

11   Zhang Juwei, and Cai Yifei, "Forecasting China's Labor Supply and Demand and the
       Unemployment Structure in the 13th Five-Year Plan Period," *Population Research* 40,
       1(2016): 38–56.

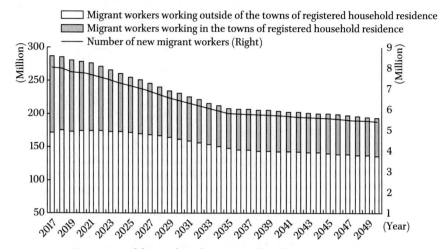

FIGURE 1.5   Projections of the number of migrant workers from 2017 to 2050 and the annual
increase

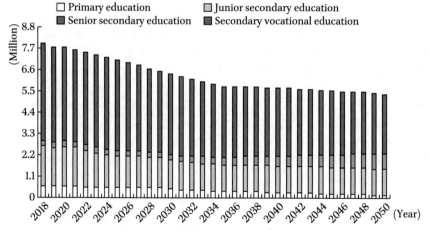

FIGURE 1.6   Annual projections of new migrant workers by educational attainment from 2018
to 2050

of migrant workers in China in 2018 in this research is 284.75 million, with a
deviation of 0.4 percent from the actual value, showing a satisfactory simulation result. Projections show that in the fourteenth FYP period, the supply
of migrant workers in China will keep declining from 286 million in 2018 to
250 million in 2025. The annual increase in the number of migrant workers is also forecasted to drop from 7.97 million in 2018 to 5.4 million in 2050.
The share of new migrant workers in new entrants to the labor market will
also fall from 57.38 percent in 2018 to 41.88 percent in 2050. While a drop is

forecasted in the number of migrant workers in China, overall the human capital of China's migrant workers will improve thanks to the rapid development of vocational education. According to the projections, the share of new migrant workers who have received at least senior secondary education will increase from 70.4 percent in 2018 to 71.8 percent in 2050.

1.2 Projections of Labor Demand during the Fourteenth FYP Period and in the Short and Medium Term

1.2.1 Projections of the Total Labor Demand

The formula for calculating total employment is $E_t = E_{t-1}(1 + \varepsilon_t g_t)$ where E stands for total employment, ε for employment elasticity, g for economic growth rate, and e × g for employment growth rate. The annual net increase in labor demand is thus $\triangle E_t = E_t - E_{t-1}$. As shown in the formulae, the key to the projection is to determine the future ε and g.

China's GDP per capita in 2018 was 9,780 US dollars, approximately the level of the US in late 1960s, Japan in mid 1970s, and the Republic of Korea (ROK) in late 1990s. In view of the gap, China is still undergoing industrialization, and its economy and employment will continue to grow at a medium-high rate for some time. If China's annual economic growth rate remains 6.5 percent, by 2030, China's GDP per capita will be around 18,000 US dollars, approximately the level of Japan in 1990 and the ROK in 2010. But China's employment elasticity is lower than that of Japan. It is estimated that the mean value of China's employment elasticity from 1978 to 2017 is 0.122, and the figure is even lower in the twenty-first century. The years between 1978 and 2017 are divided into two periods in this research for study of China's employment elasticity, i.e., before and after China's accession to the World Trade Organization (WTO) in 2001, and before and after the global financial crisis in 2008. It is estimated that China's employment elasticity is around 0.186 from 1978 to 2001 and drops to 0.029 between 2002 and 2017; the figure is 0.156 from 1978 to 2008 and drops to around 0.034 between 2009 and 2017. Based on the estimation of China's employment elasticity after the year 2000, this research uses 0.03, China's employment elasticity in 2017, as the initial value for projection, and presumes that China's employment elasticity remains at this level in 2050.

Among the factors affecting China's future economic growth, overcapacity, government debt and so on will hinder China's economic growth and cause a continuous decline in its economic growth rate. This research uses interpolation for projection of China's economic growth. To avoid the impact of macroeconomic uncertainties, we examined three levels of economic growth in view of China's economic growth rate of 6.8 percent in 2018, the projected economic growth rate of 6.5 percent in the first half of 2019 and China's shift in

TABLE 1.1   China's employment elasticity in different periods

Variable	Model I	Model II	Model III	Model IV	Model V
	1978–2017	1978–2008	2009–2017	1978–2001	2002–2017
Logarithm of	0.122***	0.156***	0.0338***	0.186***	0.0294***
GDP per capita	(15.45)	(17.03)	(15.52)	(16.91)	(42.92)
Constant term	10.02***	9.769***	10.89***	9.558***	10.94***
	(145.09)	(132.19)	(467.27)	(115.00)	(1553.99)
N	40	31	9	24	16
adj. R–sq	0.859	0.906	0.972	0.925	0.992

Note: The figure inside the bracket is the t-value.
$*p < 0.05$; $**p < 0.01$; $***p < 0.001$.

economic development from high speed to high quality in the new economic normal. For the high level of economic growth, China's economic growth rate is presumed to be 6.8 percent from 2019 to 2024, 6.5 percent from 2025 to 2029, 6.3 percent from 2030 to 2034, and 6 percent after 2035. The figures for the medium level in the same periods are respectively 6.5 percent, 6.2 percent, 6 percent, 5.8 percent and 5.6 percent. For the low level of economic growth, the economic growth rate drops by one percentage point on an annual basis. The details of the three levels of economic growth are shown in Table 1.2. During the fourteenth FYP period, the annual increase in labor demand corresponding to the three levels of economic growth is projected to be respectively 1.54 million, 1.47 million and 1.3 million or so. By 2050, China's annual increase in jobs will be 1.4 million, 1.5 million and less than one million if its economy grows at the medium, high, and low growth rate as mentioned.

1.2.2   Projections of the Structure of Labor Demand

According to the projections of economic growth and population, China's GDP per capita will reach 18,000 US dollars in 2030. That is approximately the level of the US in 1980 and Japan in 1990 when the ratio of the three sectors of economy in these two countries was respectively 4:30:66 and 7:33:60. Following the same trend, the share of employment in agriculture in China will keep declining, while the share of employment will remain stable in the

TABLE 1.2   Projections of increase in jobs from 2018 to 2050 based on employment elasticity of economic growth

Year	Employment elasticity of economic growth	High economic growth rate (%)	Medium economic growth rate (%)	Low economic growth rate (%)	Increase in jobs at high economic growth rate (ten thousand)	Increase in jobs at medium economic growth rate (ten thousand)	Increase in jobs at low economic growth rate (ten thousand)
2018	0.03	6.8	6.5	6.5	158.39	151.40	151.40
2019	0.03	6.8	6.5	6.4	158.71	151.69	149.36
2020	0.03	6.8	6.5	6.3	159.03	151.99	147.31
2021	0.03	6.8	6.5	6.2	159.36	152.29	145.24
2022	0.03	6.8	6.5	6.1	159.68	152.58	143.17
2023	0.03	6.8	6.5	6	160.01	152.88	141.08
2024	0.03	6.8	6.5	5.9	160.33	153.18	138.98
2025	0.03	6.5	6.2	5.8	153.57	146.39	136.86
2026	0.03	6.5	6.2	5.7	153.87	146.67	134.74
2027	0.03	6.5	6.2	5.6	154.17	146.94	132.60
2028	0.03	6.5	6.2	5.5	154.47	147.21	130.45
2029	0.03	6.5	6.2	5.4	154.77	147.49	128.29
2030	0.03	6.3	6	5.3	150.30	142.99	126.12
2031	0.03	6.3	6	5.2	150.59	143.25	123.94
2032	0.03	6.3	6	5.1	150.87	143.51	121.74
2033	0.03	6.3	6	5	151.16	143.77	119.54
2034	0.03	6.3	6	4.9	151.44	144.03	117.32
2035	0.03	6	5.8	4.8	144.51	139.48	115.10
2036	0.03	6	5.8	4.7	144.77	139.72	112.86
2037	0.03	6	5.8	4.6	145.03	139.96	110.62
2038	0.03	6	5.8	4.5	145.29	140.20	108.36
2039	0.03	6	5.8	4.4	145.55	140.45	106.10
2040	0.03	6	5.8	4.3	145.81	140.69	103.82
2041	0.03	6	5.6	4.2	146.07	136.08	101.54
2042	0.03	6	5.6	4.1	146.34	136.31	99.24
2043	0.03	6	5.6	4.0	146.60	136.54	96.94
2044	0.03	6	5.6	3.9	146.86	136.76	94.63
2045	0.03	6	5.6	3.8	147.13	136.99	92.31
2046	0.03	6	5.6	3.7	147.39	137.22	89.99
2047	0.03	6	5.6	3.6	147.66	137.46	87.65
2048	0.03	6	5.6	3.5	147.92	137.69	85.31
2049	0.03	6	5.6	3.4	148.19	137.92	82.96
2050	0.03	6	5.6	3.3	148.46	138.15	80.60

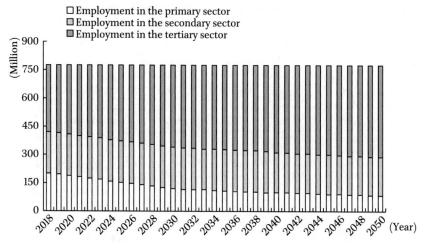

FIGURE 1.7   Employment projections by sector

manufacturing sector and gradually rise in the services sector. Considering the low starting point and large surplus population in China's agricultural sector and the major barriers to rural-urban migration in China, the share of employment in agriculture will be bigger in China than in other countries even at the same stage of development. This research presumes that the ratio of the three sectors is 15:28:57 in 2030 and that the ratio of employment in the three sectors is 10:25:65 in 2050 in China. The years in between are interpolated according to the exponential constant growth trend in 2017 and 2030, the results of which are shown in Figure 1.7.

The share of employment in non-agricultural sectors, or the secondary and tertiary sectors, can be calculated according to the projection of employment structure. Based on the projection of employment in non-agricultural sectors, the number of people employed in the base year 2017 can be projected according to the employment elasticity and economic growth in the above section, based on which the number of people employed in the following years and the number of people employed in different sectors can be calculated (See Figure 1.7). From 2017 to 2050, the number of people employed in China is projected to register an increase of 57.3 million from 766.4 million to 823.7 million. Sector wise, the number of people employed will fall from 209.44 million by around 127.07 million to 82.37 million in the primary sector, drop by around twelve million in the secondary sector, and increase by more than 186.68 million from 348.72 million to 535.4 million. Overall, the projected increase in the number of people employed in China in 2050 is not significant. The change in labor demand is mainly demonstrated through the redistribution of employment across sectors. The number of people employed in the secondary sector does not change dramatically, while the tertiary sector experiences considerable employment growth. The surplus labor from the agricultural sector and new entrants to the labor market will mainly be employed in the tertiary sector.

1.3 *Projections of China's Labor Market during the Fourteenth FYP Period and the Short and Medium Term*

This section analyses the gap between labor supply and demand in China during the fourteenth FYP period and in the short and medium term based on the above projections of labor supply and demand. While the projections of labor supply and demand are based on the total working-age population, the labor supply in practice is also affected by labor force participation rate. The current labor force participation rate in China is 68.72 percent,[12] which may continue to decline in the following years. In this section, however, for the convenience of calculation, we presume that the participation rate will remain unchanged till 2050. In addition, in China's unemployment statistics, the unemployed refers to jobless people in urban areas. In other words, rural areas are not considered in unemployment statistics. Therefore, in our analysis of the gap between labor supply and demand, the urban labor supply and new entrants to the urban labor market are calculated according to the projected urbanization rate and the total labor supply and new entrants of the country.

1.3.1 Equilibrium Is Projected between Labor Supply and Demand in China in the Fourteenth FYP Period

The number of unemployed people in urban areas is calculated based on the difference between the number of non-agricultural jobs and urban labor supply. The number of non-agricultural jobs ΔEt is calculated according to the projection of labor demand by sector in the above section, and the urban labor supply ΔUt is obtained by multiplying the working-age population in China and the urbanization rate. The formula for calculating the number of unemployed people in urban areas, ΔLt, is: $\Delta Lt = \Delta Ut - \Delta Et$.

According to the projections in Figure 1.1 and Table 1.2, the number of unemployed people in China's urban areas from 2018 to 2050 is projected (see Table 1.3). The projections show that the labor demand and supply in China will by and large be in equilibrium from 2018 to 2030, and the number of unemployed people will be negative in the fourteenth FYP period, suggesting

12 United Nations, Department of Economic and Social Affairs, "2019 Revision of World Population Prospects," https://population.un.org/wpp/.

a shortage of labor. The labor supply is projected to be slightly greater than the number of new jobs from 2018 to 2021, but the difference between labor demand and supply is less than 100,000 in 2018 and less than 10,000 from 2019 to 2021, suggesting minor employment pressure in the labor market. The employment pressure will remain small for ten years till the labor supply exceeds the labor demand in 2030 because of the declining growth of labor demand as a result of economic slowdown.

Starting from 2030, the labor supply in China will exceed labor demand, resulting in an increase in the number of unemployed people from 1,323,900 in 2030 to 5,735,400 in 2050. The peak value after 2030 is projected as more than 6.2 million in 2040. The projections further demonstrate that in the next decade, the major problem for China's labor market is no longer inadequate supply. In view of the diversification of China's economic structure and market and the increasingly serious structural problem with labor demand in its labor market, the key to development is to maintain the core competitiveness of China's economy by improving the quality of its workforce and production technology.

TABLE 1.3   Projections of urban unemployment

Year	New jobs	Labor supply (medium level)	Number of unemployed people	Unemployment rate (%)
2018	827.18	833.66	6.48	0.01
2019	836.74	837.26	0.52	0.00
2020	839.79	840.32	0.53	0.00
2021	842.84	842.85	0.01	0.00
2022	845.90	844.82	−1.08	0.00
2023	848.97	846.16	−2.82	0.00
2024	852.05	846.86	−5.19	−0.01
2025	849.44	847.03	−2.41	0.00
2026	852.38	846.82	−5.57	−0.01
2027	855.34	846.22	−9.11	−0.01
2028	858.30	845.21	−13.09	−0.02
2029	861.26	843.83	−17.43	−0.03
2030	779.95	912.33	132.39	0.20
2031	321.08	910.21	589.13	0.87
2032	322.02	907.93	585.92	0.86
2033	322.96	905.47	582.51	0.85

TABLE 1.3   Projections of urban unemployment (*cont.*)

Year	New jobs	Labor supply (medium level)	Number of unemployed people	Unemployment rate (%)
2034	323.90	902.79	578.89	0.84
2035	320.69	900.00	579.31	0.84
2036	321.60	897.01	575.41	0.83
2037	322.51	893.91	571.40	0.82
2038	323.42	890.68	567.25	0.81
2039	324.34	887.30	562.96	0.80
2040	325.25	951.83	626.58	0.88
2041	321.91	947.99	626.08	0.88
2042	322.79	944.03	621.25	0.87
2043	323.67	939.93	616.25	0.86
2044	324.56	935.47	610.91	0.85
2045	325.44	930.73	605.29	0.83
2046	326.33	925.76	599.43	0.82
2047	327.23	920.58	593.35	0.81
2048	328.12	915.20	587.08	0.80
2049	329.02	909.47	580.45	0.79
2050	329.91	903.46	573.54	0.77

Unit: 10,000

Note: The unemployment rates are the number of unemployed people divided by the economically active population in the year concerned. The projected unemployment rate from 2019 to 2023 is 0.00. That means, judging from the quantity of labor supply and demand, the demand and supply of labor in China's labor market are currently in equilibrium. The practical surveyed urban unemployment rate in 2018 in China was five percent, according to the NBS of China. The difference between the practical unemployment rate and the projected rate is a further illustration of the serious structural problem in China's labor market.

1.3.2   Groups Having Difficulties Finding Jobs

In the labor market, there is a declining demand for jobseekers with low levels of human capital due to age, lack of experience and so on. These people are thus at a disadvantage in competition for jobs, and they are referred to as groups having difficulties finding jobs. The development of other countries shows that different groups of people may have difficulties finding jobs at different stages of economic development. In Europe, for example, due to scarcity of new job opportunities ensuing from economic stagnation, a great number of young people are semi-employed or long-term unemployed. In China, many workers laid off in the reform of stated-owned enterprises in late 1990s, who were in their forties or fifties, had difficulties finding new jobs due to inability to understand and use new technologies.[13] Groups having difficulties finding jobs generally include people with disabilities, senior or long-term unemployed people, members of urban zero-employment households, workers from poor rural households, low-skilled workers with limited education and so on.

Migrant workers are typical groups having difficulties finding jobs. Due to the great mobility of migrant workers working outside of the towns of registered household residence, it is difficult to obtain accurate statistics about their unemployment, so the unemployment rate of such migrant workers is estimated based on population census data. The one-per-thousand sample survey in the sixth national population census shows that the unemployment rate of migrant workers working outside of the towns of registered household residence is 2.56 percent.[14] This low unemployment rate is in line with our observation that the unemployment rate of migrant workers working outside of their hometowns is lower than that of local urban residents. According to the *Migrant Workers Monitoring Survey Report* issued by the NBS, migrant workers employed outside the towns of registered household residence that year totaled 173 million. The number of unemployed migrant workers is thus calculated to be 4,428,800 by multiplying the number by the aforementioned unemployment rate of 2.56 percent.

The demographic structure of the unemployed from 2018 to 2050 is projected based on the above analysis of unemployment of people in their forties and fifties, college graduates and migrant workers and the projections of unemployed people (see Table 1.4). Presuming that the share of people aged over forty, college graduates and migrant workers in the unemployed is respectively sixty percent, eighteen percent and twenty-two percent, and that their shares remain unchanged between 2018 and 2050, the number of unemployed people aged over forty, unemployed college graduates and unemployed migrant workers in China will respectively reach 3.44 million, 1.03 million and 1.26 million by 2050.

13   Zeng Xiangquan, and Li Lilin, "Policy Support for Employment in Chinese Labor Market," *Journal of Renmin University of China*, 1(2003).

14   Qu Xiaobo, "Employment and Unemployment in China," in *China's Population Issue in Development: A Collection of Theses on National Population Census in 2010*, (Beijing: China Statistics Press, 2014).

TABLE 1.4   Groups having difficulties finding a job in unemployed people in urban areas

Year	Unemployed people in rural areas	People aged over forty	College graduates	Migrant workers
2018	6.48	3.89	1.17	1.42
2019	0.52	0.31	0.09	0.11
2020	0.53	0.32	0.10	0.12
2021	0.01	0.01	0.00	0.00
2022	−1.08	−0.65	−0.20	−0.24
2023	−2.82	−1.69	−0.51	−0.62
2024	−5.19	−3.11	−0.93	−1.14
2025	−2.41	−1.45	−0.43	−0.53
2026	−5.57	−3.34	−1.00	−1.23
2027	−9.11	−5.47	−1.64	−2.01
2028	−13.09	−7.85	−2.36	−2.88
2029	−17.43	−10.46	−3.14	−3.84
2030	132.39	79.43	23.83	29.13
2031	589.13	353.48	106.04	129.61
2032	585.92	351.55	105.46	128.90
2033	582.51	349.51	104.85	128.15
2034	578.89	347.34	104.20	127.36
2035	579.31	347.59	104.28	127.45
2036	575.41	345.24	103.57	126.59
2037	571.40	342.84	102.85	125.71
2038	567.25	340.35	102.11	124.80
2039	562.96	337.78	101.33	123.85
2040	626.58	375.95	112.78	137.85
2041	626.08	375.65	112.70	137.74
2042	621.25	372.75	111.82	136.67
2043	616.25	369.75	110.93	135.58
2044	610.91	366.55	109.96	134.40
2045	605.29	363.17	108.95	133.16
2046	599.43	359.66	107.90	131.87
2047	593.35	356.01	106.80	130.54
2048	587.08	352.25	105.67	129.16
2049	580.45	348.27	104.48	127.70
2050	573.54	344.12	103.24	126.18

Unit: 10,000

2   Major Problems in China's Labor Market in the Fourteenth FYP
       Period and in the Short and Medium Term

The latest statistics issued by the NBS of China show that, at the end of July 2019, China's surveyed urban unemployment rate was 5.3 percent, up by 0.2 percentage points from the level of June 2019, while the economic growth rate was projected to be 6.5 percent. As China's economy faces growing downward pressure, the pressure to stabilize employment is also mounting. Nonetheless, our analysis in the above section reveals that the demand and supply of labor in China is by and large in equilibrium, especially during the fourteenth FYP period. The major challenge for employment stability in the new situation is the structural problem in employment. For one thing, the rapid development of AI and other new technologies has raised the demand for high-quality human capital and created many service industries that adapt to new technologies. In addition to better coordinating new economies with the labor market and boosting employment flexibility, measures should be taken to ensure the basic rights of workers. For another, due to long-term weak correlation between China's rapid economic growth and employment growth, its economic growth does not play a big part in boosting employment. In addition, over eighty percent of the people employed in the agricultural sector need to be transferred to other sectors in order to narrow the productivity gap between the three sectors for sustainable development of China's economy. Therefore, further efforts are required to accelerate industrial structure upgrade and promote high-end consumer services to improve the job creation capacity of the services sector and rebalance the supply and demand in China's labor market.

The Central Economic Work Conference in July 2018 specified employment stability as the top priority for the government in pursuing stability on six fronts.[15] It demonstrates that the labor market concerns China's top decision makers more than official statistics show. According to statistics, in 2018, 13.61 million new urban jobs were created in China, up by 100,000 from the previous year. China's registered urban unemployment rate hit a new low in a couple of years at 3.8 percent at the end of 2017, and fluctuated between 4.8 percent and 5.1 percent in the second half of 2018. Contradictory to official statistics, news about massive layoffs had appeared on the Internet since early 2018. Many multinational companies announced massive layoffs in China. For example, General Motors, Ford and Ikea planned to lay off 14,700 employees, 25,000 employees and 7,500 employees respectively in China. Emerging

---

15   Stability on six fronts refers to stability in employment, finance, foreign trade, foreign
      investment, domestic investment, and expectations.

Internet companies such as Alibaba and Jingdong also announced layoff plans. How large is the employment pressure in China at present and in future?

2.1   *Facts about Official Employment Statistics*

Employment is an economic barometer. To deal with economic slowdown and ensure people's wellbeing, it is important for policymakers to reduce unemployment. Currently, there are two official indicators of unemployment in China, namely registered urban unemployment rate and surveyed urban unemployment rate. For a long time, the authorities in China have only published the registered urban unemployment rate. The surveyed urban unemployment rate was not officially published until 2018 after five years of trials.

The registered urban unemployment rate mainly reflects the situation of people who have registered their unemployment status with employment authorities. However, a greater share of the unemployed, especially the jobless migrants in urban areas, do not register. This leads to severe data distortion, and the registered urban unemployment rate has long been criticized by many parties. This indicator mainly serves as a basis for urban employment authorities when they provide unemployment benefits and job-hunting guidance to the unemployed. But this function faces a challenge from China's household registration reform. The registered unemployed people in China are mostly urban residents with local household registration. With more than 240 million migrants and 170 million migrant workers employed outside of the towns of registered household residence in China, migrants with no local household registration, especially migrant workers, are often denied access to unemployment benefits, a basic social benefit, which are based on registered unemployment. As China continues to work for equitable access to public services, there is a growing demand for improvement of the social security system covering permanent population. With improvement of the management system for urban permanent population, the registered urban unemployment rate will be gradually phased out.

The surveyed urban unemployment rate is the share of the surveyed unemployed people in the sum of the surveyed employed people and the surveyed unemployed people. It reflects the employment situation in a more accurate and scientific manner than the registered unemployment rate. This indicator also facilitates comparison with other countries. China's surveyed urban unemployment rate in December 2018 was 4.9 percent, higher than in the United States and Japan. Statistics show that the unemployment rate was approximately 3.9 percent in the United States and 2.4 percent in Japan in 2018. In that year, the US economy was buoyant and its labor market was also prosperous. Japan's unemployment rate hit a new low in nearly two decades in

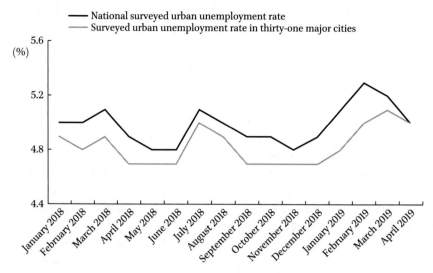

FIGURE 1.8   Surveyed urban unemployment rate in China from 2018 to 2019

2018. In Europe, on the other hand, the economic recovery was hampered by disintegration, and the unemployment rate in Europe in 2018 was about eight percent according to the World Bank.

A comparison of China's registered and surveyed urban unemployment rates in 2018 and 2019 reveals increasing employment pressure in the labor market in recent years. The accuracy of the surveyed unemployment rate is yet to be tested, but it will be used in more and more areas because of the considerable discrepancy between the registered unemployment rate and the feelings of market participants. The surveyed unemployment rate should be more widely used to track the changes in China's labor market.

Apart from possible data deviation, the difference between official unemployment statistics and the feelings of market participants is also caused by the use of a single data index. On the possible replacement of workers by new technologies such as AI and robots in China, there have been a lot of discussions, but there is no consensus. The reason is that the use of new technologies leads to higher requirements for workers. China used to rely on its cheap labor force to promote manufacturing, and is now shifting from mere increase in size to high quality growth. To be specific, in upgrade of the manufacturing industry, workers performing labor-intensive tasks that require low levels of skill are replaced by machines, and a large number of skilled workers and new talents are required. Many traditional industries and jobs begin to disappear, while new economies are creating new forms of employment and jobs. Therefore, unemployment pressure mainly comes from regional inadequacy.

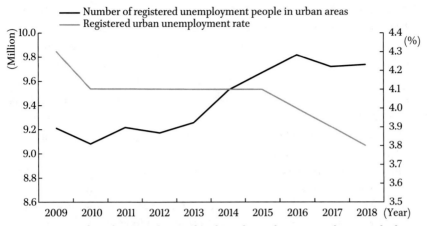

FIGURE 1.9   Number of registered unemployed people in urban areas and registered urban
            unemployment rate in China from 2009 to 2018

2.2   *Understanding China's Employment Pressure*

The registered unemployment rate in China shows a seasonal increase in unemployment. It is high in February and March when migrant workers return to work in urban areas after the Spring Festival and in July and August when fresh college graduates start looking for jobs. A comparison of the statistics of 2018 and 2019 shows that the unemployment rates in each month of 2019 were higher than their counterparts in 2018. The government faces great challenges in achieving its policy goal of full employment.

Employment is heavily dependent on economic growth. The increasing unemployment risks are closely related to China's stage of development. China is now at a critical stage of economic restructuring. Before 2010, the Chinese government's goal of economic efforts was to maintain an economic growth rate of at least eight percent. However, since its labor market reached the Lewis Turning Point and the country started industrial structure transformation and upgrade, China's economic growth rate has remained below seven percent since 2015. Its economic growth rate was 6.6 percent in 2018, and may fall to below 6.5 percent in the first half of 2019. After the global financial crisis in 2008, protectionism has been on the rise in international trade, and China has been transforming itself from the world's factory to a country of high-quality manufacturing. Developed countries may achieve full employment at an economic growth rate of three percent. But China is facing a significant increase in employment pressure as its economic growth shifts gear from high speed to medium-high speed and its economic growth rate dropped from eight percent to 6.5 percent.

China's economic growth rate in 2018 was 6.6 percent, the lowest in twenty-eight years. The economic downward pressure is even greater in 2019. The profits of industrial enterprises have been declining since the end of 2018. Statistics show that the profits of industrial enterprises in China dropped by 1.3 percent in November 2018 and 1.9 percent in December 2018, compared with the same period in 2017. In the meanwhile, the PMI of China's manufacturing industry remains below fifty percent, the threshold that separates contraction from expansion. These deteriorating indicators are heralds of increasing economic growth pressure in 2019.

Besides the increasing economic downward pressure, the structural reform in China is also a cause of unemployment. An example is the supply-side reform in 2015 to cut overcapacity, reduce excess inventory, deleverage, lower costs, and strengthen areas of weakness to deal with inefficient growth. In the process, a vast number of zombie enterprises were closed and overcapacity of some traditional manufacturing industries was eliminated, resulting in unemployment. The National Development and Reform Commission (NDRC), along with eleven other departments, issued the "Notice on Disposal of the Debts of Zombie Enterprises and Enterprises with Overcapacity" in late 2018, requiring that all debts should be dealt with by the end of 2020. This notice also deals with assistance to employees of these enterprises.

Another cause of China's increasing employment pressure is the changes in the external environment. The most important factor is the trade friction between China and the United States. After the friction broke out in 2018, many exporters rushed into massive export in the fourth quarter that year in the hope of shipping their products to the United States before the tariffs were raised in early 2019. Many people thus believed that the China-US trade friction would not have much impact on China. However, the restrictions on Huawei and other Chinese multinational companies imposed by the United States in the first half of 2019 show that China is suffering an increasing loss because of the trade friction. The China-US trade consultations have entered a critical stage, and failure to reach an agreement would mean an escalation of friction, in which case the United States may shift its focus in trade friction from tariffs to finance. Meanwhile, as the World Bank and the International Monetary Fund have both cut the global economic growth forecast for 2019, China's new economies are facing more challenges.

2.3 Challenges for China in Maintaining Employment Stability in the New Era

China faces great challenges achieving full employment in the new normal. Challenges mainly come from the following problems:

First, low employment elasticity in China due to chronic economic growth driven by capital investment. Regarding China's rapid economic growth without corresponding employment growth, some researchers believe that macroeconomic policies tend to direct investment into industries with low employment density, thus significantly undermining the effect of counter-cyclical measures on boosting employment.[16] Statistics show that China's employment elasticity has been declining since the start of reform and opening-up. It is estimated that China's employment elasticity was 0.423 between 1982 and 1990, but after 1990, it has remained around 0.1 to date. Township and village enterprises were the major source of economic growth in China from 1982 to 1990. With strong job creation capacity, the thriving township and village enterprises expedited the transfer of rural labor force to other sectors. In the 1990s, however, these enterprises gradually languished, and as foreign investment was allowed in China, the country embraced the capital intensive, investment-driven growth model. Capital-based enterprises need more capital than labor, which is the main cause of declining employment elasticity in China.

In terms of the industrial structure, the service sector takes up seventy percent in developed countries, while in China, the share is currently a bit more than fifty percent. Moreover, the primary sector contributes only seven to eight percent of China's GDP, but the people employed in this sector account for twenty-seven percent of the total, and the labor productivity in this sector is much lower than in other sectors. The people employed in China's service sector account for forty-five percent of the total, which is about the level of the United States and the United Kingdom one century ago. Currently, China's service sector comprises mainly traditional service industries. Barriers to entry in service industries relating to finance, culture, healthcare and education are generally very high, resulting in sluggish development of consumer service industries and hindering the expansion of the service sector in China.

Second, mismatch between the economic structure and the labor force structure. The development and use of AI, robots and other new technologies in recent years lead to higher requirements for human capital. National population censuses and sample surveys in China reveal the average years of schooling of rural workers as less than eight years, about eighty percent of the national average and sixty percent of the mean years of schooling of those employed in non-agricultural sectors. Among China's rural population, the level of human capital of those aged below thirty barely reaches the national average, and the average years of schooling of those aged fifty and above is less

---

16   Cai Fang, Du Yang, and Gao Wenshu, "Employment Elasticity, NAIRU and Macroeconomic Policies," *Economic Research Journal*, 9(2004), 18–25, 47.

than eight years for men and less than seven years for women. Such human capital structure cannot satisfy the requirements for workers in modern non-agricultural sectors.

Despite the improvement of overall educational attainment of China's migrant workers, the educational gap between migrant workers and urban residents with local household registration has been widening. Unlike their predecessors most of whom have at most completed junior secondary education, the bulk of new migrant workers have completed junior or senior secondary education and even obtained a bachelor's degree. It is estimated that half of the new migrant workers in China in 2018 have received secondary vocational education. The share of college graduates in migrant workers is also increasing. In 2018, college graduates accounted for about ten percent of China's rural migrants, and college-graduate-turned migrant workers totaled thirty million. College graduates with rural household registration have become an important part of migrant workers in China. Nonetheless, the tertiary education enrollment rate of teenagers with urban household registration is significantly higher. Many cities require that migrants should have at least a bachelor's degree to secure local household registration. As a result, the human capital levels of people with urban household registration have been rising faster, further widening the human capital gap between migrant workers and people with urban household registration.

China now has a migrant population of more than 240 million, including 170 million migrant workers working outside of the towns of registered household residence and their children or parents living with them. Migrant workers mainly concentrate in traditional labor-intensive service and manufacturing industries. Industrial transformation and upgrade accelerate the replacement of low-skilled, labor-intensive and repetitive jobs largely performed by migrant workers, and the use and innovation of new technologies such as AI and robots expedite economic restructuring. Workers who can adapt to new technologies will benefit from such trend, enjoy better employment quality and receive a pay rise, while those who cannot will face risks of losing their jobs.

Third, hidden unemployment in the agricultural sector. China's unemployment statistics, including registered and surveyed ones, are all about urban unemployment. Rural unemployment is not included in its surveys of unemployment, because since the founding of the People's Republic of China, policymakers and many researchers have subconsciously regarded retreating to rural areas as a last resort for migrants. It is believed that these people could at least meet their basic needs in rural areas in case of a sudden setback in urban development. Consequently, rural population are not covered in unemployment registration and surveys of unemployment. They are not covered in the government's social security system providing unemployment benefits or job training. Even migrant workers living permanently in urban areas are excluded from the urban social security system due to lack of local household registration.

Rural population's access to land also contributes to the difficulty in gathering statistics about rural unemployment. Unlike proletariats working in urban areas, rural population with access to land, no matter it is for self-use or leasing, can make a living out of their land if they become unemployed. In this regard, it should be noted that the transfer of rural labor to other sectors has not caused much change in the small-scale agricultural operation of China's rural households. Latest statistics show that, on average, each rural Chinese household has access to 0.67 hectares of cropland, which is about one third of the land available to smallholders (two hectares) according to the World Bank.[17] In 2018, the primary sector contributed only 7.2 percent to China's GDP, while employment in the sector accounted for 26.1 percent of the total. It demonstrates that amid China's rapid growth in the past years, the decline in the share of the agricultural sector in its GDP is not accompanied by accelerated transfer of rural labor. This results in a widening labor productivity gap between the three sectors. The income gap between people employed in the three sectors is also enlarged because of the large population involved in distribution in the agricultural sector.

Due to the continuous decline in agricultural labor productivity, low-income rural population are more vulnerable to poverty in exchange in a market economy. As the urban-rural gap in education, healthcare and other public services continues to grow, it has been difficult to increase the human capital investment in rural areas. The skills of the rural workforce cannot keep pace with the spread of new technologies. Moreover, the unemployed and precariously employed in rural areas tend to be excluded from observations about unemployment. Currently, China's permanent rural population stands at 580 million, including 260 million employed in the agricultural sector. There are no detailed statistics about these people concerning their employment status and ability to meet their basic needs, but visits in rural areas show that part-time and temporary jobs are commonplace. According to the definition of employment, people working part-time and temporarily should be considered unemployed. Based on China's surveyed urban unemployment rate of five percent (though the actual rural unemployment rate may be higher), the number of jobless people in China's rural areas is about thirteen million.

---

17   Cai Fang, "Urbanization in the New Era," *International Economic Review*, 4(2018).

3   Main Conclusions and Policy Recommendations

Overall China is facing increasing pressure due to the structural mismatch in employment. The long-term weak correlation between rapid economic growth and employment growth suggests that the social value created by production and services is not enjoyed by the whole workforce. This not only has an impact on income distribution, but also affects stability of the labor market. Meanwhile, the development of new technologies increases employment flexibility in the labor market, intensifying the mismatch between human capital and job requirements. In response to structural unemployment risks arising from economic restructuring and frictional unemployment in the process of adapting to new technologies, efforts are required to enhance the job creation capacity of industries, and structural reform should be performed on the supply side of labor to improve the skills and capabilities of the workforce. During the process, while the efforts to rebalance employment have a host of goals, high labor force participation rate and low unemployment rate are crucial to economic and social stability and development.

3.1   *Rebalancing Demand and Supply of Labor for Full Employment*
Due to information asymmetry in the market and regional imbalances in development, there is a gap between jobs and labor demand in different sectors and regions. To balance demand and supply in the labor market, the government needs to take proactive employment measures to rebalance the labor market across sectors and regions. For full employment under the pressure of economic downturn, efforts are also required to pursue stability of and improvement in labor force participation rate, improve the allocative efficiency of capital and labor, and increase labor productivity.[18]

In view of China's overall employment level, to ensure full employment, it must keep the surveyed urban unemployment rate below 5.5 percent. Apart from unemployment rate, the speed of urbanization, the number of working-age population and labor force participation rate are also indicators of employment stability. In China, the retirement age is currently fifty-five for women and sixty for men. Currently the retirement age in China is fifty-five for women and sixty for men, so, the number of people in need of jobs can be calculated based on the number of the working-age population. Statistics show that there

---

18   Du Yang, "Where to Start to Ensure Employment Stability," *Economic Daily*, February 26, 2019, page 12.

were about 900 million people aged between sixteen and fifty-nine in China in 2018, accounting for 64.3 percent of the country's total population. Based on China's monthly average of surveyed urban unemployment rate, 4.9 percent, providing that China can keep its surveyed unemployment rate below 5.5 percent in 2020, it is projected that China will be able to maintain employment stability with about 1.65 million new jobs in 2020 while its working-age population is shrinking and it is pressing ahead with urbanization.

A low unemployment rate alone may enable a balance between labor supply and demand, but neglect of the declining labor force participation rate will lead to decrease in human capital efficiency. High-quality employment policies are introduced to achieve employment goals in an ideal situation with high labor force participation rate and low unemployment rate. The co-existence of a low unemployment rate and a low labor force participation rate indicates that in a labor market in near-equilibrium, a large share of the labor force are not economically active. It is a waste of human resources. Therefore, in addition to controlling the surveyed urban unemployment rate, the efforts to maintain a healthy and stable labor market should have a higher goal: maintaining and increasing the labor force participation rate.

Considering from the perspective of price signals in the labor market, a steady increase in wages is also an important goal for boosting labor supply and labor productivity. Rising wages are a reflection of economic growth and an important indicator of improved labor welfare. For the labor demand side, however, rise in wages means higher costs, and when it outpaces demanders' profits growth, businesses, especially labor-intensive ones, are bound to be hit. It is evident that a strong correlation exists between wage increase and rebalancing in the labor market.

The rapid increase in wages in China is partly caused by economic growth, but structural labor shortage also plays an import role. Since 2013, the working-age population aged between sixteen and fifty-nine in China have been declining, which alleviates the country's employment pressure, but intensifies structural labor shortage. Technological advances change the skills and capabilities required of the workforce, and exacerbate the structural conflict between supply and demand in the labor market. Such structural labor shortage is driving up wages. It is also noteworthy that the disconnection between rise in wages and labor productivity results in rising unit labor cost. In an increasingly uncertain external economic environment, export-oriented enterprises and sectors face greater difficulties achieving employment stability. Therefore, for more stable full employment in the long run, efforts must be made to coordinate the supply and demand of labor and labor costs in the market.

3.2 Dealing with Different Types of Unemployment to Rebalance the Job Market

The design of proactive employment policies is based on the degree of unemployment risks. An accurate understanding of different types of unemployment and groups facing unemployment risks is essential for targeted policy design.[19] From the perspective of economic efficiency, the government needs to either achieve its policy goals at minimum administrative cost, or create an optimal employment situation with existing government expenditure.

Employment in economics is divided into cyclical unemployment, structural unemployment and frictional unemployment. Cyclical unemployment is caused by a decline in jobs due to insufficient aggregate demand in a cyclical economic downturn, structural unemployment results from economic restructuring, and frictional unemployment is mainly caused by information asymmetry in the labor market and so on. In China which is at a critical stage of supply-side economic reform, the unemployment is primarily structural, but there is also frictional unemployment resulting from changes in labor market institutions. It is thus necessary to adopt measures in response to different types of unemployment to rebalance the job market.

There are two causes of structural unemployment. The first is shifts in resource allocation. Due to frequent international trade frictions and increasing economic downward pressure in China, the labor cost in the country is rising fast. If resources can move freely, the gap between regions in terms of returns on capital and labor will narrow, thus reducing the gap between regions and sectors in marginal returns. Inefficient businesses and industries will be eliminated or downsized, while efficient regions or sectors will be strengthened. The movement of labor is more likely to be hindered by geographical or administrative factors than that of capital. The elimination of businesses and the downsizing of industries inevitably leads to job losses, thus causing structural unemployment. The second cause of structural unemployment is the replacement of labor due to use of technologies in some businesses and industries in the wake of changes in the external environment, such as productive transformation of industries thanks to technological advancement. A pronounced feature of structural unemployment is its concentration in certain regions, industries and businesses, on which proactive employment policies shall be based. Specifically, in economic restructuring, attention should be paid to the development of micro, small and medium-sized enterprises. While it is important to understand that the superseding of micro and small

---

19   Du Yang, "Understanding Unemployment of Different Natures and Improving Coordination of Employment Policies," *21st Century Business Herald*, April 15, 2019, page 4.

enterprises is normal in economic development, the government must pay attention to the impact of economic uncertainty on the development of small and medium-sized enterprises. It is recommended that funds and subsidies for stabilizing and boosting employment shall be combined with policies supporting the development of micro and small enterprises. An important measure to prevent structural unemployment is to assist affected employees of eliminated zombie enterprises.

Frictional unemployment is mainly caused by a mismatch between labor demand and supply. Examples include seasonal unemployment in the agricultural sector and unemployment of pregnant women. Since frictional unemployment is largely temporary, comparing with its effect on overall employment, policymakers and researchers are often more concerned about the impact of such temporary unemployment on livelihoods of the unemployed and providing them with policy support. The rapid development of new economies and technologies and the industrial restructuring and upgrade in China in recent years have resulted in the disappearance and upgrade of jobs at a faster pace. As it takes time for workers to adapt to new technologies and jobs, temporary unemployment during the process is getting increasingly serious. To reduce frictional unemployment in a market economy, China needs a more flexible labor market and more employment information platforms. Efforts should be made to improve people's jobhunting ability and reduce job search costs for individuals. It is also necessary to provide on-the-job training and improve the existing vocational training to help workers better satisfy the new requirements posed by new technologies at a faster pace.

CHAPTER 2

Source of Domestic Demand: Measuring Migrants' Consumption Potential in the New Era

Cheng Jie* and Yin Xi**

1   Migrants: Workers or Consumers?

The reform and opening-up started an era of industrialization and urbanization in China. Rural workers swarm into cities. The labor force move faster between urban and rural areas, between regions, and between cities. The labor market is taking shape, and the number of migrants in the country has been on the rise. Statistics from national population censuses show that China's migrants increased at an annual growth rate of more than eight percent from 6.57 million in 1982 to 221 million in 2010. According to the NBS of China, in 2017, the number of people who live in places other than their towns of registered household residence in China reached 291 million, of which 244 million were migrants. Since the start of the new era, China's demographic and economic structures have been changing at a faster pace. In 2011, China saw the first net decrease in the size of its working-age population, or people aged between fifteen and fifty-nine, which means that the demographic dividend supporting the country's rapid economic growth is gradually tapering off. China has become a middle-income country, and its economic growth is gradually slowing down. The growth rate of migrants in China has decreased significantly, and the size of the migrant population is leveling off. According to *Migrant Workers Monitoring Report 2018* issued by the NBS, the total number of migrant workers in China reached 288 million, but its growth rate dropped to 0.6 percent, close to zero; the number of migrant workers employed outside the towns of registered household residence was 173 million, and its growth rate dropped to 0.5 percent; the number of migrant workers employed outside their home provinces decreased by 1.1 percent compared with the previous year.

Migrants' consumption behavior in receiving places has been intensively studied. The primary motivations for migration are jobs and income. However, migrants do not have equal access to public services and social security like

---

*   Cheng Jie is an associate professor at the Institute of Population and Labor Economics, CASS, and his research interests are social security and employment.

** Yin Xi is a graduate student at the Graduate School of Chinese Academy of Social Sciences.

urban residents due to urban-rural divide and restrictions on household registration. As a result, the level and characteristics of migrants' consumption are different from that of urban residents. Many researches reveal that migrants' consumption level is significantly lower than that of urban residents,[1] and that the coverage of old age insurance, health insurance and other social security programs has an impact on migrants' consumption.[2] There have also been a lot of researches on migrants' remittance. Migrant workers send the bulk of their income to their hometowns. With a small share of income spent on consumption in urban areas where they work, migrant workers' consumption expenditure is mainly incurred in their hometowns. Most researchers agree that remittance accounts for a large proportion of migrant workers' income.[3] Therefore, it has long been a consensus that in receiving places of migrants, migrants' consumption demand is insufficient, and their marginal propensity to consume (MPC) is low.

More importantly, as China enters a new stage of economic development, it is advancing new urbanization at a faster pace, thus ushering in a new phase of urbanization. The consumption demand of both urban and rural residents reaches a higher level, and migrants' consumption behavior is showing new characteristics. Since the start of the new era, China's decision-making authorities have attached more importance to integrated urban-rural development, the household registration reform has made substantial progress, and accelerated efforts have been made to ensure equal access to basic public services. Migrants in China have gradually settled in cities with stable jobs. The migration pattern is also changing from individual migration to household migration. As significant changes are taking place in both macroeconomy and the lives of individuals, migrants' consumption behavior is also changing. In addition, the Chinese economy is now at a critical stage of shifting growth drivers and development model, and domestic demand is an important booster for China's future economic transformation and upgrade. Considering the low consumption level of migrants in receiving places due to the current urban-rural divide,

1   Chen Binkai, Lu Ming, and Zhong Ninghua, "Household Consumption Constrained by Hukou System," *Economic Research Journal*, supplement (2010), 62–71; Wang Meiyan, and Cai Fang, "Destination Consumption Enabling Migrants' Propensity to Consume," in eds. *China's Transformation in a Global Context*, Song Ligang, Ross Carnaut, Cai Fang, and Lauren Johnston (Australia: ANU Press, 2015), 91–110.

2   Yang Cuiying, and Wang Runquan, "The Impact of Urban Social Security on Consumption by Floating Population," *Shanghai Journal of Economics*, 12(2016), 97–104; Song Yueping, and Song Zhengliang, "The Promoting Effect and Its Mechanism of Health Insurance on the Migrants' Consumption," *Population and Economics*, 3(2018), 115–126.

3   Sheng Yinan, "Family Migration in China," *Population Research*, 4(2013), 66–79; Xu Qi, and Zou Hong, "Job Stability and Urban-to-rural Remittance in China: A Test of Co-insurance Theory," *Population and Development*, 1(2016), 38–48.

granting permanent urban residency to migrants can help unleash migrants' consumption potential, which will drive the country's economic transformation and development. It is thus necessary to continuously conduct basic research on migrants' consumption behavior in the new era.

The China migrants dynamic survey (CMDS) is an annual national sample survey conducted by the National Health Commission of China (the former National Health and Family Planning Commission) starting from 2009. The survey combines comprehensive and thematic approaches. The comprehensive survey is a nationwide continuous cross-sectional monitoring survey of migrants and their family members about their basic information, style and trend of migration, employment, social security, income and expenditure, housing conditions, access to basic public health services, administration of marriage and family planning services, migration and education of children, psychological and cultural conditions and so on. The survey is conducted in places in thirty-one provincial units and Xinjiang Production and Construction Corps with a heavy concentration of migrants. Based on the data of 1,312,169 sample households from 2010 to 2017, this research calculates the consumption level of China's migrants in the new era, and uses the income elasticity of consumption to reflect the changes in migrants' consumption behavior. The income elasticity of consumption refers to the change in percentage in consumption in response to the change in income by one percent. The formula for calculating the said elasticity is $E_y = \dfrac{\Delta C / C}{\Delta Y / Y}$, where C stands for consumption, Y for income, and ΔC and ΔY for marginal consumption and income respectively. The income elasticity of consumption measures consumers' propensity to consume at a given level of income, and reflects the changes in consumption demand caused by changes in economic development phase and residents' income.

2   Changes in Migrants' Income Elasticity of Consumption

2.1   *Trend of Migrants' Income Elasticity of Consumption*
Calculation based on data from the CMDS shows that the migrants' income elasticity of consumption is 0.672. This result is close to the calculation results obtained by Zhang et al.[4] and Yang et al.[5] in their researches. Zhang et al.

---

4   Zhang Huachu, and Liu Shenglan, "The Impacts of Unemployment Risk on Migrants' Consumption," *Economic Review*, 2(2015), 68–77.
5   Yang Cuiying, and Wang Runquan, "The Impact of Urban Social Security on Consumption by Floating Population," *Shanghai Journal of Economics*, 12(2016), 97–104.

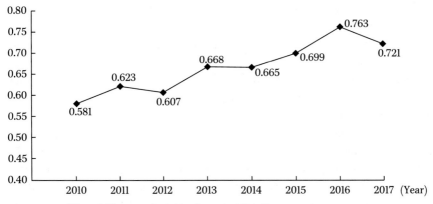

FIGURE 2.1   Migrants' income elasticity of consumption from 2010 to 2017

used the CMDS data in 2013 and calculated that migrants' income elasticity of consumption was 0.68, which is close to the figure 0.668 in 2013 shown in Figure 2.1. The figure in this research is lower than migrants' income elasticity of consumption in 2007 and 2008 calculated by Wang et al.,[6] and has a great difference from Wang's calculation results of the elasticity based on China Urban Labor Survey in 2016,[7] which can be attributed to the systematic bias caused by using data from different sources.

Figure 2.1 shows the changes in migrants' income elasticity of consumption. As shown in the figure, the migrants' income elasticity of consumption in China has remained above 0.6 since the start of the new era, and peaked at 0.763 in 2016. Overall, the migrants' consumption is income elastic. In addition, migrants' income elasticity of consumption has been rising at a fast rate and has shown an obvious upward trend in recent years.

The income elasticity of consumption of China's migrants in general has reached a high level. It is thus necessary to break the stereotype that migrants do not consume in urban areas. An increasing proportion of migrants' income is spent on consumption, while the share of savings is declining, suggesting that migrants' consumption is evidently converging with that of urban residents.

This trend is of great significance to the current efforts to expand domestic demand in urban areas. China has been striving to drive economic growth with consumption since its economy enters the new normal, and an important way

---

6   Wang Tao, and Mao Jianxin, "The Consumption Difference between Migrant Families and Urban Households: Based on Quantile Regression," *Population and Economics*, 4(2015), 60–68.

7   Wang Meiyan, "The Level and Structure of the Consumption of the New Generation of Migrants: Compared with the Old Generation of Migrants," *Studies in Labor Economics*, 6(2015), 107–126.

to do so is to unleash migrants' consumption potential. Considering migrants' high propensity to consume, their consumption level will gradually become similar to that of urban residents. Therefore, raising migrants' disposable income can effectively improve the overall consumption level. In addition, further migration of rural workers to urban areas will, apart from increasing labor supply, effectively raise the consumption level in urban areas and consequently stimulate economic growth.

Since migrants contribute to the urban economy by increasing domestic demand, they should have access to the same level of social security as urban residents. At present, however, due to their status as nonlocals and the urban-rural divide, migrants' access to social security is significantly worse than that of urban residents.[8] Household registration restrictions, income uncertainty and other factors all have a negative impact on migrants' consumption,[9] which to a certain extent hinders the efforts to unleash migrants' consumption potential. Therefore, improvement of migrants' social conditions can effectively increase their consumption.

2.2 Regional Differences in Migrants' Income Elasticity of Consumption

Migrants' income elasticity of consumption varies across regions. In general, the figure is the lowest in the east and the highest in the central region, while the west and the northeast have similar figures. In terms of migrants' average consumption and income, the regions in descending order are the eastern region, the central region, the west and the northeast. Migrants in the east have higher average income, but there is no significant difference in migrants' average consumption in these regions. It is noteworthy that the proportion of inter-provincial migration is seventy-two percent in the east, which is the highest. In the central, western and northeastern region, the figure is respectively twenty-two percent, forty-two percent and thirty-six percent. The consumption level and income elasticity of consumption of inter-provincial migrants are lower than other migrants. It is thus assumed that a larger proportion of inter-provincial migrants may reduce the income elasticity of consumption.

Table 2.1 shows the migrants' income elasticity of consumption in different places and the difference in such elasticity of the migrants in four regions of the country. The income elasticity of consumption of the migrants in four regions

---

8 Yang Juhua, "Urban-Rural Divide and Inside-Outside Disparity: Unequal Access of Migrants to Social Securities in China," *Population Research*, 5(2011), 8–25.

9 Chen Binkai, Lu Ming, and Zhong Ninghua, "Household Consumption Constrained by Hukou System," *Economic Research Journal*, supplement (2010), 62–71.

TABLE 2.1   Migrants' income elasticity of consumption in different places

Place	Income elasticity of consumption	Region	Income elasticity of consumption
Jiangsu	0.616	East	0.646
Hebei	0.628		
Zhejiang	0.639		
Shandong	0.649		
Shanghai	0.662		
Fujian	0.665		
Guangdong	0.676		
Tianjin	0.684		
Beijing	0.694		
Hainan	0.703		
Jiangxi	0.636	Central	0.675
Anhui	0.659		
Yunnan	0.680		
Henan	0.686		
Hubei	0.689		
Hunan	0.705		
Shanxi	0.708		
Tibet	0.609	West	0.659
Inner Mongolia	0.610		
Shaanxi	0.623		
Xinjiang Production and Construction Corps	0.634		
Guangxi	0.66		
Gansu	0.664		
Qinghai	0.675		
Xinjiang	0.681		
Ningxia	0.694		
Guizhou	0.695		
Chongqing	0.710		
Sichuan	0.720		
Heilongjiang	0.640		
Liaoning	0.677	Northeast	0.655
Jilin	0.687		

SOURCE OF DATA: CALCULATION BASED ON DATA FROM THE CMDS

are all relatively high. The difference between migrants of rural and urban household registration in income elasticity of consumption is significant in the east, but minor in the other three regions. The migrants' income elasticity of consumption shows different characteristics in different places. In comparison, the elasticity is relatively low in economically developed provinces such as Jiangsu, Zhejiang and Guangdong, and high in less developed provinces. In addition, the elasticity in Beijing, Shanghai, Tianjin and Chongqing, four cities which are economically developed, is relatively high, which may be attributed to migrants' higher cost of living in economically developed cities.

2.3   *Group Differences in Migrants' Income Elasticity of Consumption*

Significant differences exist between migrants of different characteristics in terms of the income elasticity of consumption. The calculation based on relevant data shows that the income elasticity of consumption of migrants of rural household registration is 0.0257 lower than that of migrants of urban household registration. When the household income per capita falls below 4,055 yuan, the consumption level of migrants of rural household registration is higher, suggesting that migrant workers' income restricts their propensity to consume. Inter-provincial migrants' income elasticity of consumption is 0.0244 lower than that of intra-provincial migrants. Inter-provincial migrants show lower propensity to consume due to difficulties in inter-provincial settlement of social insurance expenses and other obstacles. The consumption level of inter-provincial migrants is only higher than intra-provincial ones when household income per capita is below 2,398 yuan. The income elasticity of consumption of home-owning migrants is 0.0692 higher, which is probably an illustration of the inhibitory effect of the pressure to buy a home in migration destinations on migrants' propensity to consume.

The income elasticity of consumption also varies across age groups. As shown in Figure 2.2, migrants' income elasticity of consumption shows an S-shaped curve as age increases. Among the people aged twenty to thirty four, the elasticity increases with age, and the highest figure is found in the groups aged twenty-five to thirty-four. The income elasticity of consumption of middle-aged migrants decreases with age, and reaches a plateau in groups aged over forty-five, while the figure is relatively higher in the group aged over sixty.

The difference between age groups in income elasticity of consumption can be explained by the characteristics of different stages of life. Migrants in their early twenties are new entrants to the labor market, who have growing consumption capacity and demand and optimistic expectations of their future income, so their income elasticity of consumption keeps rising. Young adults aged twenty-five to thirty-four, who constitute the bulk of China's migrants,

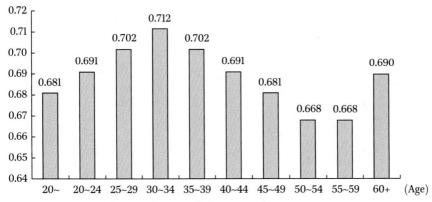

FIGURE 2.2   Migrants' income elasticity of consumption by age group

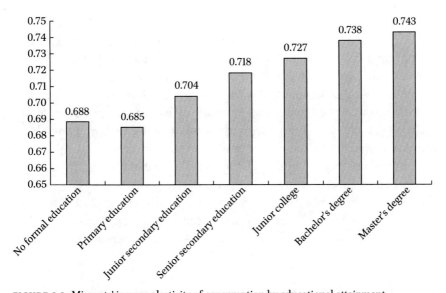

FIGURE 2.3   Migrants' income elasticity of consumption by educational attainment

spend a large proportion of their income on consumption and keep a low savings rate. People aged over thirty-five have established families, so they begin
to save for the future and lower their level of consumption, resulting in a
decrease in their income elasticity of consumption. The sixty plus age group
shows a high income elasticity of consumption because of heavier financial
burden caused by higher medical and other expenses.

Figure 2.3 shows migrants' income elasticity of consumption by educational
attainment. It demonstrates that the elasticity increases with the level of education, and that better education results in a stronger propensity to consume.
One reason is that better education enables wider horizons and consequently

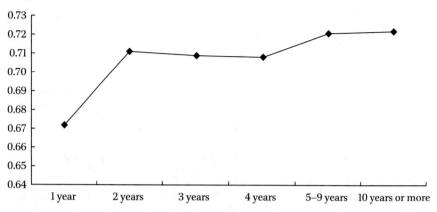

FIGURE 2.4 Migrants' income elasticity of consumption by duration of stay

access to a larger variety of consumer goods, thus increasing the likelihood of consumption. Another reason is that better-educated migrants may have lighter burdens in their lives and are more likely to consume.

The extension of migrants' stay in migration destinations also contribute to their propensity to consume. Figure 2.4 shows the changes in migrants' income elasticity of consumption as the duration of stay in destination places increases. As migrants stay longer in a place, their income elasticity of consumption is also increasing, though the annual growth is slowing down. There is a marked trend that migrants' propensity to consume is changing towards that of urban residents. The longer they stay in a receiving place, the more likely they are to consume in this place instead of keeping or transferring elsewhere a large proportion of their income in the form of savings or remittances.

3   Estimate of the Consumption Potential Unleashed by Granting Permanent Urban Residency to Migrants

Granting permanent urban residency to migrants is an important task in China's new urbanization strategy, which will ensure migrants' equal access to basic public services and benefits as local residents. In that case, the propensity to consume and income elasticity of consumption of migrants and local residents will converge. This will unlock migrants' consumption potential to the greatest extent. Based on differences in income elasticity of consumption between migrants and local residents, this study estimates the consumption potential unleashed by granting permanent urban residency to migrants, which will help people better understand the boosting effect of new urbanization on domestic demand. Calculation in the above section shows that the

TABLE 2.2 Estimated income elasticity of consumption of urban residents in China

Item	Total sample	2003	2005	2007	2009
	Logarithm of household consumption	Logarithm of household consumption	Logarithm of household consumption	Logarithm of household consumption	Logarithm of household consumption
Logarithm of household income	0.803*** (133.53)	0.830*** (76.95)	0.818*** (70.74)	0.783*** (62.20)	0.783*** (62.32)
Control variable	√	√	√	√	√
Constant term	1.278*** (26.69)	0.999*** (10.85)	1.198*** (12.20)	1.584*** (15.40)	1.411*** (13.41)
Sample size	28548	7156	7216	7232	6944

Note: The numbers inside the brackets are t-values. *** stands for ten-percent level of significance; ** stands for five-percent level of significance; * stands for one-percent level of significance. The control variables of province and year are included. Control variables are mainly demographic characteristics of individuals and households.

SOURCE: URBAN HOUSEHOLD SURVEY (UHS)

income elasticity of consumption of China's migrants is on the rise. But has it converged with that of local residents? Is there any room for further increase? To answer these questions, a unified analytical framework is required to calculate urban residents' income elasticity of consumption based on nationally representative data.

The Urban Household Survey (UHS) conducted by the NBS of China, covering households across the country except for those in Hong Kong SAR, Macao SAR and Taiwan, is the most representative sample survey of households in China. This research randomly selects 40,000 households from the data of said national sample survey from 2003 to 2009 at a one-year interval for estimation of urban residents' income elasticity of consumption. To ensure comparability, the structure of the regression model of urban residents' income elasticity of consumption is roughly the same as that of model (1), except that two control variables, duration and pattern of migration, which do not apply to local residents, are deleted. As shown in Table 2.2, urban residents' income elasticity of consumption is around 0.8 and does not change dramatically from year to year. Yang estimated that the short-term income elasticity of consumption of urban

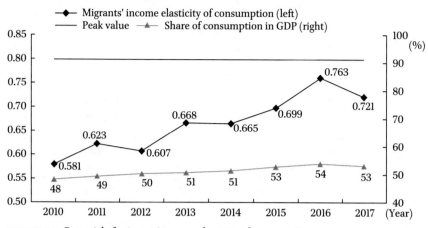

FIGURE 2.5 Potential of migrants' income elasticity of consumption

residents is 0.81,[10] which is close to the estimation results of this research, while urban residents' income elasticity of consumption from 1980 to 2008 in China is estimated to be 0.899 based on macro data.[11] The elasticity based on macro data is often higher than that based on micro data. For consistency, this research uses the figure 0.8, which is based on micro household data, as the target value of income elasticity of consumption for migrants' permanent urban residency.

With 0.8 as the target value of migrants' income elasticity of consumption (see Figure 2.5), the migrants' income elasticity of consumption in China is converging with that of urban residents, and there is still room for it to increase. In 2017, the income elasticity of consumption of migrants in China was 0.72, eight percentage points lower than that of urban residents. Economic growth driven by domestic demand is an important goal of China in the transformation of its economic development pattern. Though the contribution of consumption to China's economic growth has been on the rise since 2010, and the share of final consumption in its GDP has slowly risen from forty-eight percent to fifty-three percent, there is still a lot to be done to expand domestic demand. Currently, urban residents' income elasticity of consumption remains stable, and their consumption growth is mainly driven by income rise. Migrants' consumption, on the other hand, can be stimulated by rise in either

---

10   Yang Yongbing, "A Comparison of the Consumption Elasticity of Urban and Rural Residents based on the Error Correction Model," *Statistics and Decision*, 7(2011), 100–101.

11   Zhang Bangke, Deng Shengliang, and Tao Jianping, "On the Income Elasticity of Consumption of Urban Residents in China from 1980 to 2008," *Statistics and Decision*, 17(2011), 116–118.

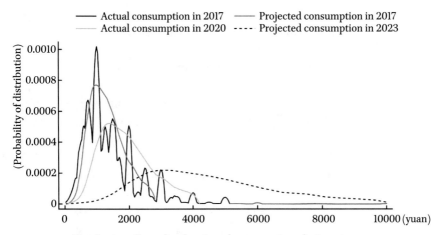

FIGURE 2.6 Distribution of actual and projected consumption of migrants

income or income elasticity of consumption. Granting permanent urban residency to migrants is of great significance to unlocking consumption potential, expanding domestic demand and advancing the transformation of economic development pattern.

The increase in income elasticity of consumption can directly stimulate consumption demand. We projected migrants' consumption potential based on the models' estimation results and economic forecasts. The basic hypotheses of the simulation are as follows:

(1) Migrants' income elasticity of consumption in 2017 is 0.72. We presumed that the elasticity will stay around 0.75 in 2020 and reach the upper limit 0.8 in 2030 when China achieves its goal of new urbanization.

(2) The per capita income of migrant households and China's GDP will grow at the same rate. For the GDP growth rate, this research uses the forecasts of the International Monetary Fund (IMF) before 2024, and presumes it to be 5.5 percent from 2025 to 2030. Based on China's constant GDP price in 2017, its GDP will reach 98.63 trillion yuan in 2020 and 169.84 trillion yuan in 2030.

(3) We presumed that the country's migrant population will remain around 244 million, and their demographic characteristics will remain stable.

Figure 2.6 shows the distribution of migrants' actual and projected consumption. The simulated values, which exclude the effect of residuals, are closer to normal distribution.

Considering migrants' enormous consumption potential, they will become an important source of domestic consumption demand. As shown in Table 2.3, in 2017, when migrants' income elasticity of consumption was 0.72 and their average income per month is 3,424 yuan, their annual consumption totaled

5.1 trillion yuan or so, accounting for 6.2 percent of China's GDP that year; in 2020, when migrants' income elasticity of consumption reaches 0.75 and average monthly income becomes 4,135 yuan, their consumption will rise to 6.7 trillion yuan, accounting for 6.7 percent of China's GDP that year; when China achieves the goal of new urbanization in 2030, migrants' income elasticity of consumption will reach 0.80, their average monthly income will rise to 7,120 yuan, and their total consumption will amount to 15.8 trillion yuan, equivalent to 9.3 percent of China's GDP that year.

TABLE 2.3   Projections of consumption potential unleashed by granting permanent urban residency to migrants

Item	2017	2020		2025		2030	
Income elasticity of consumption	0.72	0.75	0.72	0.78	0.72	0.80	0.72
Average income per month (yuan)	3424.29	4134.80	4134.80	5447.66	5447.66	7119.87	7119.87
Average monthly consumption expenditure (yuan)	1747.82	2282.81	1785.26	3652.35	2177.96	5393.96	2641.67
Total consumption expenditure of migrants (trillion yuan)	51176	66841	52273	106941	63771	157935	77348
GDP (hundred million yuan)	820754	986342	986342	1299518	1299518	1698418	1698418
Share of migrants' consumption in GDP (%)	6.20	6.70	5.30	8.23	4.91	9.30	4.55
Increase in consumption created by increase in income elasticity of consumption (trillion yuan)	/	14568	/	43170	/	80587	/
Increase in share of consumption in GDP caused by increase in income elasticity of consumption (%)	/	1.48	/	3.32	/	4.74	/

SOURCE: CALCULATION BASED ON DATA FROM THE CMDS

The growth of consumption demand comes from both income growth and the increase in income elasticity of consumption. The consumption potential of migrants who are granted permanent urban residency mainly comes from the rise in income elasticity of consumption. Assuming that migrants' income elasticity of consumption stays at 0.72 as in 2017 and only considering the expansion of consumption demand caused by income growth, we can observe the net effect of granting permanent urban residency to migrants by comparing with the simulated results in the scenario of increasing income elasticity of consumption. The simulation shows that if the income elasticity of consumption in 2020 remains at the level of 2017, the total consumption of migrants will rise to 5.2 trillion yuan; if the income elasticity of consumption rises to 0.75, the total consumption will increase to 6.7 trillion yuan, which is 27.9 percent higher than the scenario with unchanged income elasticity of consumption, and the share of migrants' total consumption in GDP will increase from 5.3 percent to 6.7 percent by 1.4 percentage points. If the income elasticity of consumption in 2030 remains at the 2017 level, the total consumption of migrants will only be 7.7 trillion yuan; if it rises to 0.8, the total consumption will expand to 15.8 trillion yuan, more than twice the figure in the scenario with unchanged elasticity, and the share of migrants' total consumption in GDP will increase from 4.6 percent to 9.3 percent by 4.7 percentage points. Migrants' income elasticity of consumption plays an important role in expanding consumption, and granting permanent urban residency to migrants will unleash considerable consumption potential.

4   Conclusions and Policy Implications

China's GDP per capita reached 4,200 US dollars in 2010. According to the World Bank's standard, China has become a middle income country. In such a new phase of development, there is more room for consumption upgrading, and migrants' consumption needs will also change. This research uses nationally representative data from the CMDS from 2010 to 2017 to calculate migrants' income elasticity of consumption since the start of the new era and examine the differences in such elasticity between regions and groups. Based on the calculation results, nationally representative data from the urban household survey are used to calculate the income elasticity of consumption of urban residents and the consumption potential that may be unleashed by granting permanent urban residency to migrants. The main conclusions are as follows:

(1) Since the start of the new era, migrants' income elasticity of consumption in China has shown a significant upward trend, and has reached a high level. It was 0.67 on average from 2011 to 2017, and increased to 0.72 in 2017. Migrants show a tendency to consume in receiving places. This conclusion changes the traditional understanding of migrants' consumption behavior. Migrants are no longer people who have low propensity to consume and focus on savings and remittances.

(2) Migrants' income elasticity of consumption varies across groups. Migrants' income elasticity of consumption is lower in economically developed regions, which may be attributed to high housing prices and cost of living. Urban-to-urban migrants have higher income elasticity of consumption than migrant workers, and inter-provincial migrants have lower income elasticity of consumption than intra-provincial migrants. Migrants' income elasticity of consumption shows an S-shaped curve as age increases, and it rises gradually as the level of education and the duration of stay in receiving places increase.

(3) Migrants' income elasticity of consumption is lower than that of urban residents, so there is still room for improvement. Granting permanent urban residency to migrants has a significant boosting effect on consumption. If permanent urban residency of migrants can enable the convergence of the income elasticity of consumption of migrants and urban residents, migrants' consumption will reach 15.8 trillion yuan in 2030, equivalent to 9.3 percent of the GDP that year. The consumption growth directly created by granting permanent urban residency to migrants will be about eight trillion yuan, equivalent to 4.7 percent of the GDP that year.

The changes in migrants' income elasticity of consumption in China since the start of the new era have profound economic implications. As China has come to a new stage of economic development and urbanization, the size of its migrant population is leveling off, and the migration pattern is changing. More migrants are moving with their families. Migrants have stable jobs and live in urban areas. They come to urban areas not only for jobs, income and remittances. Instead, they spend an increasing share of their income consuming in urban areas. Migrants are increasingly similar to urban residents. They are not only a source of labor supply for urban economic development, but also important consumers. Higher income elasticity of consumption and income of migrants and further migration of rural labor to urban areas can effectively expand the consumption in receiving places and boost economic growth. To achieve these goals, efforts should be made to further improve the social security system integrating urban and rural areas, accelerate equal access to public services, and push forward with the reform of the household registration system to facilitate the transformation of migrants to urban residents and further unleash migrants' consumption potential. These efforts will have a profound impact on cities in expanding domestic demand and accelerating the transformation of economic development pattern.

CHAPTER 3

Changes in China's Labor Market from the Perspective of Changes in Labor Supply Elasticity

Cheng Jie* and Zhu Yufeng**

1   Labor Supply in Urban and Rural Areas in Economic Transformation

China's economic development since the implementation of the reform and opening-up policy has been accompanied by massive population migration. The migration of rural workers to urban areas has especially been a critical driving force for China's miraculous economic growth. Migrants in China have become important participants of the urban labor market and the primary source of new labor supply. China's economic development is characterized by a dualistic structure. In the early stage of its reform and opening-up, as modern economic sectors were developing and expanding, surplus labor moved to the emerging sectors for employment without substantial increase in their wages, giving rise to a dualistic economy. A huge number of surplus rural labor, whose marginal output was nearly zero, migrated to urban areas. Migrants were able to improve their livelihoods simply by moving from the agricultural sector to non-agricultural sectors.[1] The urban labor market enjoyed a nearly unlimited supply of rural labor. Rural-to-urban workers largely entered the secondary labor market with long-term wage stagnation. A steady flow of new rural workers migrated to urban areas even though their wages were not raised, and a very slight rise in wages could significantly motivate workers. During this period, the migrants' wage elasticity of labor supply was close to infinite. In the early 1980s, without any significant increase in output per person employed (GDP per person employed), employment in China expanded rapidly. According to macro indicators, the elasticity of overall labor supply in China during this period was about 0.4, and that of non-agricultural labor

*   Cheng Jie is an associate professor at the Institute of Population and Labor Economics, CASS, and his research interests are social security and employment.
** Zhu Yufeng is a graduate student of Shanghai Academy and Shanghai University.

1   Cai Fang, "Demographic Transition, Demographic Dividend, and Lewis Turning Point in China," *Economic Research Journal*, 4(2010), 4–13.

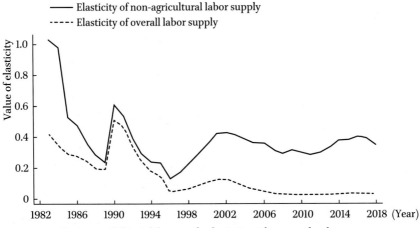

FIGURE 3.1   Estimate of China's labor supply elasticity at the macro level

supply reached 1.0 or so. Around 1990, temporary adjustments were made in the economic and reform areas in China, and the market-oriented economic reform and the reform of state-owned enterprises were in full swing, resulting in a decline in fluctuation in labor supply elasticity (see Figure 3.1).

Since the start of the twenty-first century, China's economy has maintained a steady and rapid growth, and structural changes have taken place in its labor market. The changes have been especially pronounced since 2003, as the growth of labor demand has outpaced that of labor supply, leading to rapid wage growth and labor shortage and wage convergence in the labor market. Regions and employers are competing for workers. The era with an unlimited supply of labor has come to an end, and the foundation of wage formation is gradually changing from living standards to the marginal product of labor. China has reached the Lewis Turning Point.[2] Thanks to the replacement of near-infinity supply of migrants by a relevant shortage or limited supply and the changes in migrants' response to variation in the urban labor market, further efforts to attract workers to urban areas result in a substantial increase in wages. Workers begin to base their migration and labor supply decisions on wage levels, which means that migrants' labor supply elasticity has changed from close-to-infinity to an observable positive number. The labor supply elasticity at the macro level also shows a temporary rise. While wages are growing and labor productivity is rising fast, employment, especially in urban non-agricultural sectors, increases significantly. Estimation shows that the average elasticity of non-agricultural

---

2   Cai Fang, and Wang Meiyan, "Growth and Structural Changes in Employment in Transition China," *Journal of Cooperative Economics*, 1(2010), 71–81.

labor supply increased from 0.23 between 1996 and 2000 to 0.40 between 2001 and 2005, and the average elasticity of overall labor supply rose from 0.07 to 0.10 during the same periods.

China's demographic and economic structural transformation have gathered pace and entered a new phase since 2010. With the acceleration of population ageing, the total labor supply in China has reached a turning point. According to the NBS of China, China's working-age population, i.e., people aged between fifteen and fifty-nine, has registered an annual net decrease of millions after it peaked at 925 million in 2011. The cumulative reduction in China's workforce from 2012 to 2018 amounted to approximately twenty-six million. Another turning point in China's labor market came in 2018 when the number of the employed dropped for the first time, which implies a downward trend irreversible in a long period of time, after peaking at 776 million. China's migrant population has also been shrinking slowly after it peaked at 253 million in 2014. The number of migrant workers employed outside their towns of registered household residence reached 170 million in 2018, but its growth rate has been slowing down to near zero. Despite the significant changes in labor supply, the wages and labor cost in China continue to grow fast. The underlying cause of the waning demographic dividend that has driven China's economic growth over a long period of time is the changes in labor supply elasticity. Wage growth can no longer directly create a steady supply of labor, and the reservoir of labor has dried up. The changes in labor supply elasticity at the macro level also show new characteristics. Estimation (see Figure 3.1) shows that the overall labor supply elasticity in China has been declining since 2010 and has dropped to about 0.03. Thanks to continued economic restructuring and urbanization efforts, the employment in China's urban areas and non-agricultural sectors have maintained a steady growth, and the elasticity of non-agricultural labor supply has shown a minor increase. Nonetheless, the elasticity of non-agricultural labor supply has also shown signs of decline in the past two years after reaching a high level of 0.4.

With the total population and workforce reaching a plateau or even declining, the only way to further increase labor supply is to raise labor force participation rate and hours of work. Labor force participation rate generally has a greater marginal contribution to labor supply than hours of work. Ceteris paribus, an increase by one percentage point in the overall labor force participation rate can lead to a rise in total labor supply by one percentage point. For example, an output elasticity of labor at 0.5 will translate into an increase of 0.5 percentage points in economic growth. This is why developed economies such as Japan and the United States pay great attention to labor force participation rate. Du and Jia (2018) estimate that the labor force participation rate of people aged sixteen to sixty-five in China dropped by 4.7 percentage points from 2010 to 2015, which resulted in a GDP decrease by 9.1 percentage points, equivalent to an annual decrease of 1.8 percentage points. But to raise the labor force participation rate is not an easy task, as it is subject to the influence of various factors, such as the level of economic development, labor market institutions, culture, perceptions and so on. Generally, as an economy develops, workers expect higher reservation wages to participate in the labor market, and labor supply elasticity tends to decline. Multiplied efforts are needed to make public policies to raise the labor force participation rate and hours of work. The practice of developed countries, however, shows that such efforts have not paid off.

Is it possible to further raise the labor force participation rate and hours of work in China in the new era? Migrants can give a better answer to this question since they are most sensitive to changes in the labor market. If the labor force participation rate and hours of work remain elastic with respect to wages, China can still maintain its labor supply in the traditional way to support its economic development. On the other hand, a significantly declining labor elasticity or potentially inelastic labor supply suggests that profound changes are taking place in China's labor market. That being the case, the effect of increasing labor supply on economic growth will keep decreasing, and it will be increasingly difficult to maintain a steady economic growth by directly expanding labor supply. Under the circumstances, economic growth can only be achieved by improving labor productivity, and the drivers for economic development need to be changed from traditional input of factors to productivity improvement. This is an illustration of the new normal of the economy.

Changes in migrants' labor supply elasticity will shed some light on China's economic development in the new era. While China is changing from a middle-income country to a high-income one, will wage growth continue to motivate migrants to participate in the labor market or increase their working hours? This study uses nationally representative survey data to estimate the elasticity of labor force participation and working hours, and examines the changes in migrants' labor supply in response to a new stage of economic development and changes in the labor market since the start of the new era.

2 Labor Supply in the Transition from a Dualistic Economy to a Neoclassical Economy

2.1 Theoretical Hypothesis

The labor supply decision of individuals is a function of income (consumption) and leisure. It demonstrates the sense of satisfaction individuals can derive from a specific level of income (consumption) and leisure. The labor supply decision and the hours of work rest with the substitution effect and the income effect caused by wage changes. If the substitution effect is stronger, individuals tend to increase their labor supply to earn income or to consume. If the income effect is stronger, individuals tend to do less work and have more leisure to gain utility. The labor supply curve depicts the relationship between the price of labor, i.e., wages, and labor supply. In labor economics, there is a backward-bending labor supply curve. When wages are low, individual workers tend to supply more labor as their wages increase, resulting in dominance of the substitution effect and a positive elasticity of labor supply. When wages reach a higher level, individual workers tend to value leisure above labor supply, causing stronger income effect than the substitution effect and a negative elasticity of labor supply.

China's economy is undergoing transformations in various fields. As the transition from a planned economy to a market economy and the change from urban-rural divide to urban-rural integrated development are both well underway in China, its labor supply curve may be more complicated and show a host of characteristics. To better understand the characteristics of china's labor supply curve and the changes in labor supply elasticity, the labor supply curve is expanded to include four stages (see Figure 3.2).

The labor supply elasticity in the first stage is close to infinity. In the early stage of development of the urban-rural dual economy dominated by agriculture, the supply of rural labor is close to infinity, and there is a vast number of surplus rural labor in the agricultural sector with close-to-zero marginal output. The rural level of wages is determined by the average product, not marginal product, of rural labor. That is to say, rural wages are institutional wages covering people's essential needs for survival. As urban wages (Wu) exceed rural institutional wages (Wr), the agricultural sector serves as a source of labor supply with infinite elasticity for modern sectors in urban areas.

The labor supply elasticity in the second stage is positive and remains great. As modern sectors in urban areas continue to expand, the labor demand curve gradually moves rightward from D1 to D2, and the growth of labor demand outpaces that of labor supply. The surplus rural labor force has been absorbed by different sectors in urban areas, and the supply of labor is no longer unlimited. The marginal product of rural labor changes from zero to positive and starts to rise, but it is still lower than wages in modern urban sectors. As shown in the section from A to B in the labor supply curve, the expanding urban sectors continue to absorb rural workers. It suggests that the first Lewis Turning Point (A) has come, after which the labor supply is no longer infinite, wages begin to go up, and the labor supply curve begins to slope upward to the right, but the supply elasticity remains great.

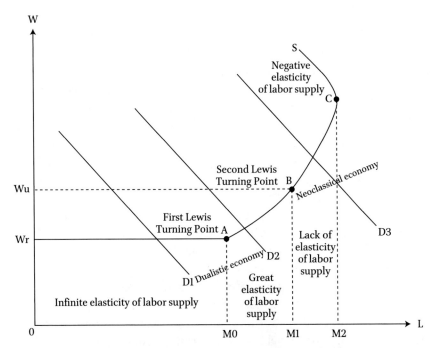

FIGURE 3.2 Four-stage hypothetical labor supply curve in the transition from a dualistic economy to a neoclassical economy

In the third stage, the labor supply elasticity is still positive, but its value becomes lower. Urban sectors continue to expand, and the marginal product of labor in the traditional agricultural sector and modern urban sectors becomes the same. A labor market integrating urban and rural areas is established, and the dualistic economy comes to an end, suggesting the arrival of the second Lewis Turning Point (B). Urban and rural workers base their labor supply and migration decisions on unified wage levels. The labor supply curve slopes upward and becomes steeper. The substitution effect of wages on labor supply decreases, while the income effect becomes stronger, and the elasticity of labor supply falls significantly and approaches zero.

In the fourth stage, the elasticity of labor supply becomes negative. The economy reaches a higher stage of development, urban and rural residents have a higher level of needs and attach more importance to consumption and leisure. Economic development relies more on productivity improvement. Wage growth tends to motivate workers to work less and have more leisure, so the income effect of wages on labor supply exceeds the substitution effect. As shown in Figure 3.2, the labor supply curve bends backward at C, and the labor supply elasticity turns from a positive number to a negative one.

2.2   *Empirical Strategy*

According to Heckman (1993), changes in labor supply include variation in the labor market in terms of both extensive and intensive margins. Changes in the extensive margin refer to variation in labor force participation or employment, and those in the intensive margin mean changes in working hours of people in work. A study of the variation in labor supply shall deal with both labor force participation and working hours. In empirical studies, labor supply elasticity is usually understood as the changes in working hours in response to wage variation, i.e., the wage elasticity of working hours. But labor force participation is actually more sensitive and important to the labor market than working hours (Heckman, 1993). This paper studies migrants' labor supply behavior in the context of China's transition from a dualistic economy to a neoclassical economy, and examines the response of migrants' labor supply behavior to the price in the labor market from the perspectives of labor force participation rate and working hours.

Based on classic labor supply theories, the empirical analysis uses the model of labor supply decision to represent the labor supply behavior of individuals with labor force participation and working hours, i.e., by constructing the labor force participation model and the labor supply model.

2.3   *Data*

This study uses the CMDS data from 2011 to 2017. The CMDS is an annual national sample survey conducted by the National Health Commission of China (formerly the National Health and Family Planning Commission) starting from 2009. The survey combines comprehensive and thematic approaches. The comprehensive survey is a nationwide monitoring survey of migrants and their family members about their basic information, style and trend of migration, employment, social security, income and expenditure, housing conditions, access to basic public health services, administration of marriage and family planning services, migration and education of children, psychological and cultural conditions and so on. The survey is conducted in places with a heavy concentration of migrants in thirty-two provincial units and Xinjiang Production and Construction Corps. This study uses the data from the comprehensive surveys of the CMDS from 2011 to 2017, with 120,000 to 200,000 migrant household samples each year and a total sample size of 1.2 million households. The respondents' employment and income and the characteristics of individuals and households are combined with city-level indicators to estimate migrants' labor supply elasticity.

Based on data from the one-percent national population sample survey in 2005, consistent model structures and estimation methods are used to estimate the elasticity of labor force participation and working hours of migrants and urban residents in 2005, thereby examining the changes in migrants' elasticity of labor supply. The data from the said population sample survey in 2005 are used because they are nationally representative and include wages as an indicator. Other population censuses and one-percent national population sample surveys do not contain such information, so their data cannot be used to estimate labor supply elasticity. For data analysis, this study randomly selects 2,585,481 subsamples, which are twenty percent of the original samples, including 273,687 migrants, and 602,012 urban residents of non-agricultural household registration.

2.4 Selection of Variables and Descriptive Statistics

The key explained variables are labor force participation rate and hours of work. According to data from the CMDS from 2011 to 2017, the average labor force participation rate of migrants is eighty-seven percent, and migrants work 57.1 hours per week on average, more than the statutory working hours per week, forty-four hours, in China. These people migrate mainly for jobs, so they show a strong propensity to work and a high labor force participation rate, and their work intensity is relatively higher. In 2005, the average labor force participation rate of migrants and urban residents in China was seventy-eight percent and sixty-three percent respectively, with an increase in migrants' overall labor force participation rate, which was significantly higher than that of urban residents. The migrants' average working hours per week was also significantly longer than urban residents. All these show that, with other conditions remaining the same, the potential for further increase in migrants' labor supply is relatively limited.

The core explanatory variable is the wage level of individuals, which is used to estimate the impact of changes in hourly wage on labor force participation and working hours of individuals. According to data from the CMDS, the average hourly wage of migrants in China was 18.7 yuan from 2011 to 2017, with a pronounced upward trend. The number reached 23.5 yuan in 2017, an increase of 112 percent from the level of 2011, with an average annual growth rate of 13.3 percent. The one-percent national population sample survey in 2005 showed that the average hourly wage of migrants and urban residents in China was respectively 6.3 yuan and 6.5 yuan. In 2017, the average wage of the country's migrants increased by 2.7 times from the level of 2005, registering

TABLE 3.1   Descriptive statistics of major variables: based on data from the CMDS from 2011 to 2017

Variable	Definition	Standard deviation	Minimum value	Maximum value	Mean value
LFP_ind	Employed (Yes: 1; no: 0)	0.34	0	1	0.87
working_hours_ind	Working hours per week	16.85	1	140	57.07
wage_hour	Hourly wage (yuan)	10.24	3.33	174.81	18.67
prgdp	Real GDP per capita	86309	112	931453	46799
unemp_city_2010	Urban unemployment rate in 2010	2.40	0.01	24.75	5.83
gender_i	Gender (Male: 1; female: 0)	0.50	0	1	0.54
age_i	Age	10.06	16	100	35.73
edu	Educational level	3.02	0	19	9.86
hukou_i	Household registration (Agricultural: 1; non-agricultural: 0)	0.36	0	1	0.84
style_i	Style of migration (inter-provincial: 1; intra-provincial: 0)	0.50	0	1	0.51
duration_i	Duration of migration (year)	5.14	1	82	6.00
size	Household size	1.19	1	10	2.54
age_avg	Average age of household members	10.04	7.40	94	31.31
cdr	Children dependency ratio	0.36	0	5	0.26
edr	Elderly dependency ratio	0.14	0	4	0.02

an average annual growth rate of 11.6 percent. Since the start of the new era, migrants in China have seen rapid wage growth, but their labor force participation rate and working hours have remained stable, which to a certain extent reflects the changes in supply and demand in the labor market. Migrants' labor supply behavior appears to be not very sensitive to variation in wages.

The control variables fall into four areas. The first type is about demand, namely the real GDP per capita and the surveyed unemployment rate of the cities concerned, which reflect the level of economic development and labor market performance. We calculated the surveyed unemployment rate of cities using micro data from population censuses or one-percent national population sample surveys. The average surveyed unemployment rate of the sample cities in 2010 was 5.8 percent, higher than the average, three percent, in 2005. The second type is about characteristics of individuals, such as gender, age, educational level, household registration, and style and duration of migration. The data from the one-percent national population sample survey in 2005 do not contain information about duration of migration. The third type is about household characteristics, such as household size, average age, children dependency ratio (children aged sixteen and younger), elderly dependency ratio (people aged sixty and older). The fourth type is about place and time, or specifically, the province and the year concerned.

3   Declining Labor Supply Elasticity

3.1   *Estimate of Overall Labor Supply Elasticity*
The elasticity of labor force participation and labor supply of migrants in China in general is significantly positive. The labor supply decisions of average workers are still responsive to wage levels in the labor market. The estimates of the Heckman two-step model show that the estimated coefficient of working hours is 0.083, which is significant at the one-percent level. In other words, a growth of one percent of hourly wage corresponds to an increase of 0.083 percent in migrants' hours of work. It shows that, ceteris paribus, wage growth in the labor market still has a significant impact on migrants' labor supply and continues to motivate them to participate in the labor market and increase their working hours. The labor supply curve of migrants is in the third stage of the transition from a dualistic economy to a neoclassical one, and the elasticity of labor supply has not turned negative.

As shown in Table 3.2, the estimated results of main control variables have all passed the significance test. Demand factors are not considered in most micro-level labor supply models. The estimated coefficient of real GDP per capita is significantly negative, suggesting that in cities with better developed economies, migrants are less likely to participate in the labor force and tend to work fewer hours, and that the income effect in the theoretical hypothesis is playing a role. The estimated coefficient of the surveyed unemployment rate reflecting the situation in the labor market is negative, suggesting that in cities fitting expectations and with high unemployment rates, migrants have greater difficulty in finding jobs, lower willingness to participate in the labor force, and work fewer hours due to underemployment. The estimated results of other individual- and household-level control variables also have implications. The estimated coefficient of household registration is positive, reflecting higher

TABLE 3.2   Estimates of the models of overall labor force participation rate and working
             hours: based on data from the CMDS from 2011 to 2017

	LFP Probit	ln_wh Heckman
w_i_p	0.529***	0.0829***
	(0.00433)	(0.00702)
ln._prgdp	−0.000902**	−0.00746***
	(0.000444)	(0.000672)
unemp_city_2010	−0.00198***	−0.000991***
	(0.000177)	(0.000277)
gender_i	0.0550***	−0.0194***
	(0.000990)	(0.00226)
age_i	0.00129***	−0.000338***
	(0.0000487)	(0.0000933)
hukou_i	0.0947***	0.0562***
	(0.00152)	(0.00152)
style_i	0.0140***	0.0210***
	(0.000675)	(0.00103)
edu	−0.0196***	−0.0215***
	(0.000216)	(0.000348)
duration_ind	0.000409***	0.000841****
	(0.0000610)	(0.0000912)
size	−0.0306***	0.0206***
	(0.000313)	(0.000706)
age_avg	−0.00150***	0.000670***
	(0.0000582)	(0.000104)
cdr	−0.0655***	0.0110***
	(0.00123)	(0.00214)
edr	0.0457***	−0.0147***
	(0.00212)	(0.00376)
Province	Yes	Yes
Year	Yes	Yes
Obs.	938914	943814

Note: (1) The estimated coefficient of hourly wage is the marginal effect in the model of labor
force participation, and the value of elasticity in the model of working hours. (2) Inside the
brackets are the standard errors of the regression. *** stands for significance at one-percent
level, ** for significance at five-percent level, and * for significance at ten-percent level. (3) Yes
means that the relevant variables are controlled in model estimation.

labor force participation rate and longer working hours of migrants with agricultural household registration than those with non-agricultural household registration. Inter-provincial migrants have higher labor force participation rate and labor supply level than intra-provincial migrants. Longer duration of migration leads to greater job security, and has a positive effect on labor force participation rate and labor supply. Children dependency ratio has a negative effect on migrants' labor force participation rate and a positive effect on their working hours. Elderly dependency ratio, on the other hand, has a positive effect on migrants' labor force participation rate and a negative effect on their working hours.

3.2   *Changes in Labor Supply Elasticity*

Migrants' labor supply elasticity shows an obvious downward trend. Based on consistent model structures, the estimation based on data from the one-percent national population sample survey in 2005 (see Table 3.3) shows that the marginal effect of wage levels on migrants' labor force participation in 2005 reached 1.23, suggesting that migrants were very sensitive to wage signal in the labor market. It also shows that migrants' labor force participation elasticity dropped sharply from 2011 to 2017, during which the marginal effect fell to 0.53, as shown in the overall model estimation. In addition, since the start of the new era, migrants' labor force participation elasticity has been constantly declining. The model estimation results by year show that the estimated marginal effect of the labor force participation model dropped from 0.71 in 2011 to 0.40 in 2017. The effect of wage changes in the labor market on migrants' labor force participation decisions is waning, and migrants' behavior is becoming less sensitive to such changes.

The wage elasticity of working hours is also declining. The estimation based on the data from the one-percent national population sample survey in 2005 shows that migrants' working hours was still elastic, and the value of elasticity reached 0.15. That means, for every one-percent increase in wages, migrants' working hours increased by 0.12 percent. From 2011 to 2017, the elasticity of working hours dropped to 0.08. The migrants' elasticity of working hours in this period also shows a downward trend. The model estimation by year reveals fluctuations from year to year in the value of elasticity of working hours, but in general, the elasticity value was decreasing and dropped to 0.07 in 2017. Workers were less motivated by wage growth to increase their hours of work. It is expected that the income effect of wage growth will gradually increase, and workers will put more and more emphasis on leisure and quality of life.

The significant decline in the elasticity of labor force participation and working hours means that the slope of migrants' labor supply curve tends to become steeper, and that the labor supply curve is going through the third stage or moving towards the fourth stage. The variation in labor supply elasticity reflects profound changes in China's labor market over the past decade or so. With an increasingly ageing population and a declining working-age population, the potential for migrants to further increase their labor supply is dwindling. The labor force participation elasticity of migrants is significantly lower than that of urban residents. The estimates based on data from the one-percent national population sample survey in 2005 show that the marginal effect of urban residents' labor force participation is 2.93, while the elasticity of working hours of migrants and urban residents are similar (see Table 3.3).

TABLE 3.3   Estimates of the models of labor force participation and working hours: based on data from the one-percent national population sample survey in 2005

	Migrant		Urban resident	
	LFP Probit	ln_wh Heckman	LFP Probit	ln_wh Heckman
w_i_p	1.231***	0.150***	2.928***	0.145***
	(0.0190)	(0.0164)	(0.0279)	(0.0130)
ln_prgdp	0.00274*	−0.00707***	−0.00646***	−0.00535***
	(0.00141)	(0.00103)	(0.00154)	(0.000875)
unemp_city_2005	−0.0103***	0.00279**	−0.0148***	0.00643***
	(0.00105)	(0.000893)	(0.00102)	(0.000692)
gender_i	−0.0337***	0.00626	−0.234***	−0.0539***
	(0.00419)	(0.00614)	(0.00453)	(0.00430)
age_i	−0.00948***	−0.00190***	−0.0324***	−0.00279***
	(0.000153)	(0.000146)	(0.000261)	(0.000144)
hukou_j	0.419***	0.111***		
	(0.00569)	(0.00512)		
style_i	0.0473***	0.0403***		
	(0.00232)	(0.00294)		
Edu	−0.100***	−0.0269***	−0.302***	−0.0431***
	(0.00183)	(0.00162)	(0.00322)	(0.00168)
size	0.0200***	0.00238***	−0.00683***	0.00966***
	(0.000648)	(0.000253)	(0.000734)	(0.000728)
age_avg	−0.00174***	−0.000624***	−0.00308***	−0.000599***
	(0.000175)	(0.000154)	(0.000157)	(0.000900)

TABLE 3.3   Estimates of the models of labor force participation and working hours (*cont.*)

	Migrant		Urban resident	
	LFP	ln_wh	LFP	ln_wh
	Probit	Heckman	Probit	Heckman
cdr	−0.0963***	−0.00509	−0.0378***	−0.0553***
	(0.00336)	(0.00274)	(0.00363)	(0.00468)
edr	−0.0323***	−0.00980	−0.0143***	0.0700***
	(0.00443)	(0.00830)	(0.00332)	(0.00529)
Obs.	189515	201708	346025	386052

Note: (1) The estimated coefficient of hourly wage is the marginal effect in the model of labor force participation, and the value of elasticity in the model of working hours. (2) Inside the brackets are the standard errors of the regression. *** stands for significance at one-percent level, ** for significance at five-percent level, and * for significance at ten-percent level.

4   Conclusions and Implications

Migrants are an important source of supply for China's urban labor market. Thanks to their heavy concentration in market-oriented sectors, they are more sensitive to changes in the labor market. Estimates of migrants' labor supply elasticity can shed some light on China's stage of economic development and changes in its labor market in the new era. This study combines the wage equation with the model of labor supply decisions to estimate the elasticity of labor force participation and labor supply based on nationally representative data from the CMDS from 2011 to 2017 and the one-percent national population sample survey in 2005. The study reveals a significant downward trend in migrants' overall labor force participation elasticity in China since the start of the new era. The marginal effect of migrants' overall labor force participation on wage levels decreased from 1.23 in 2005 to 0.40 in 2017, and averaged 0.53 between 2011 and 2017. Migrants' labor force participation decisions are increasingly less responsive to wage changes in the labor market. The wage elasticity of working hours is also declining. Migrants' wage elasticity of working hours was 0.15 in 2005, but it dropped to 0.08 from 2011 to 2017. Workers are less motivated by wage growth to work more hours, reflecting rapid changes in China's labor market.

China has witnessed profound changes in its demographic and economic structures, and it has entered a new stage of economic development. Since the implementation of the reform and opening-up policy, the Chinese economy has been growing rapidly. Since the start of the twenty-first century, China's economy has been integrated into the global economy at a faster pace, and the demand for labor in its urban areas has been rising rapidly at a growth rate higher than that of labor supply. China is gradually undergoing a transition from a dual structure with unlimited supply of labor (in which case the elasticity of labor supply is infinite) to relative shortage of labor. The country has reached the Lewis Turning Point, which means that the transfer of labor from traditional sectors to modern sectors must be accompanied by a steady increase in wages, and that the labor supply elasticity starts to be positive. As China becomes an upper middle-income economy, the demand of urban and rural residents is also upgraded, and migrants attach more importance to consumption and leisure and better quality of life in addition to wage growth. The stimulating effect of wage growth on migrants' labor force participation rate and working hours is decreasing. China is undergoing a transition from a dual economy to a neoclassical economy. It is shifting away from the traditional factor-driven pattern of economic development and relies more on improvement in labor productivity and total factor productivity.[3] During such transition, the contribution of labor supply to economic growth will be gradually replaced by that of technological progress. In the context of structural changes, the significant decline in the elasticity of labor force participation and hours of work of migrants in China implies that the labor supply curve tends to become steeper.

The changes in migrants' labor supply elasticity have important implications for China's economic development and changes in the labor market in the new era. The potential for increase in migrants' labor force participation rate and working hours through wage growth keeps shrinking. In the new era, China's urban labor market is seeing profound changes in the demand and supply of labor, and factors other than the labor price is needed to expand of the labor market. It is foreseeable that the urban labor market will remain tight, the increase in labor supply will play a limited role in driving the sustainable development of urban economy, and the internal pressure for transition towards economic development driven by productivity improvement is mounting. Migrants are more responsive to changes in the economic environment

---

3   Cai Fang, "How Can Chinese Economy Achieve the Transition Toward Total Factor Productivity Growth," *Social Sciences in China*, 1(2013), 56–71.

and the labor market, but our estimation shows that the elasticity of migrants' labor force participation is significantly lower than that of urban residents. Considering the current labor supply and demand, the migrants' labor supply potential has almost been fully tapped. Further efforts to increase labor supply shall mainly focus on urban residents.

CHAPTER 4

Reallocation of Human Capital: Productivity Divergence across Sectors

*Qu Yue**

1 Improvement in Labor Productivity Is the Fundamental Path to Future Economic Development

China's economic growth in the past decades has largely been driven by the rapid development of its manufacturing industries, especially labor-intensive ones. The fast development of traditional labor-intensive manufacturing industries is known to benefit from the demographic dividend thanks to the good supply of labor in a dualistic economy, and from allocative efficiency improvement following the migration of rural labor to modern industrial sectors in urban areas.[1] Thanks to the huge demographic dividend, China's manufacturing industries enjoy the advantage of low labor costs, which in turn drives the rapid growth of the entire Chinese economy. Changes have taken place in China since it became a middle-income country, including the disappearing demographic dividend and the moderate increase in resource and environmental costs due to reform of the factor market, and some deep-rooted structural problems have emerged. China can no longer maintain a steady economic growth with the previous inefficient development pattern which emphasizes scale and speed and which is driven by input of labor, capital and other factors. There is very limited potential for improving the allocative efficiency relying on traditional demographic dividend and reallocation between agricultural and non-agricultural sectors. The new sources of growth can only

---

* Qu Yue is an associate professor at the Institute of Population and Labor Economics, CASS, and her research interests are labor economics and employment.

1 Gary H. Jefferson and Jian Su, "Privatization and Restructuring in China: Evidence from Shareholding Ownership," *Journal of Comparative Economics*, 34(2005), 146–166; Loren Brandt, Changtai Hsieh, and Xiaodong Zhu, "Growth and Structural Transformation in China," in Loren Brandt and Thomas G. Rawski, *China's Great Economic Transformation*, (New York: Cambridge University Press, 2008), 683–728; Shenggen Fan, Xiaobo Zhang, and Sherman Robinson, "Past and Future Sources of Growth for China," EPTD Discussion Paper No. 53.

be found in productivity improvement and a higher level of human capital required in the upgrade of traditional low-end industries to high-end ones.

2 Characteristics of the Industrial Structure and Productivity in an Upper-Middle-Income Economy

As an economy becomes more developed, its focus shifts from the primary sector to the secondary sector, and then to the tertiary sector. While this takes place in China, since the start of reform and opening-up, the country has also seen a massive movement of labor from rural to urban areas and enjoyed a greater resource reallocation effect. Nonetheless, as China's economic development reaches a certain stage, the absolute quantity of its labor force has started to decrease, the movement of rural labor to urban areas are slowing down, and its industrial structure is undergoing a transition towards the medium and high end. The low-end labor-intensive industries in the secondary sector will gradually upgrade to capital- and technology-intensive ones. In the tertiary sector, traditional service industries will upgrade to modern high-end services represented by producer services such as financial and information services.

2.1 Comparison with Other Countries in Terms of the Stage of Development

China's economy has been growing rapidly in recent years, with its GDP per capita rising from 318 US dollars in 1990 to 9,780 US dollars in 2018. Based on gross national income per capita, the World Bank divides countries into four groups, i.e., low-income countries, lower-middle-income countries, upper-middle-income countries, and high-income countries. According to the World Bank's income classification criteria which are updated annually, China fell into the low-income group in the 1990s; in 1998, China's GDP per capita reached 829 US dollars and became a lower-middle-income country which was moving towards the upper-middle-income group; in 2010, China's GDP per capita was close to 4,561 US dollars and became an upper-middle-income country; now, China is an upper-middle-income country advancing towards the high-income group.

According to the laws of industrial development, as the gross national income per capita rises, the share of the primary sector in GDP will keep declining. Since China became a lower-middle-income country, the share of the primary sector in its GDP has been falling, which dropped to 7.2 percent in 2018, while the share of employment in China's primary sector is slightly lower than the average of upper-middle-income countries. With further progress in industrialization and the development of service industries, the share of the secondary sector in China's GDP has been rising and then declining. Although China became an upper-middle-income country in 2010, the share of the secondary sector in China's GDP remains higher than in other upper middle-income countries, while the share of employment in its secondary sector is close to the average of upper-middle-income countries. In comparison with the said two sectors, the tertiary sector, or the services sector, better reflects the economic development in the later stage of industrialization. The share of the tertiary sector in China's GDP has been rising, which reached 52.2 percent in 2018. China became an upper-middle-income country in 2010, and its service industries have been developing rapidly, but the share of the tertiary sector in China's GDP is still lower than the average of upper-middle-income countries. Since China became a lower-middle-income country, the share of employment in China's tertiary sector has been rising, but it is still lower than the average of upper-middle-income countries.

2.2   *Characteristics of the Industrial Structure and Its Changes*

It is necessary to understand the current employment structure and economic structure in China. As shown in Figure 4.1, since China started to reform and open up its economy, the share of the primary sector in China's GDP has remained stable: the share has remained low, and has been declining slightly. The share of the primary sector in China's GDP dropped from about thirty percent in 1979 to 7.2 percent in 2018, after which the primary sector hardly accounts for a major proportion of the country's GDP. Therefore, we should pay more attention to the secondary and tertiary sectors. An examination of the changes in the shares of these two sectors in China's GDP shows that China's industrial structure has experienced changes in three stages. The first stage was from 1978 to 1990, during which the share of the tertiary sector was rising, the share of the secondary sector was falling, and the former remained lower than the latter. The second stage was from 1991 to 2011, which saw fluctuations in the shares of both sectors, but overall the share of the tertiary sector continued to increase, while that of the secondary sector continued to drop slowly. The third stage came after 2012, during which the tertiary sector outdid the secondary sector in contribution to the GDP, becoming the most important part of the national economy; the gap between the tertiary sector and the secondary sector started to widen. During the thirteenth FYP period, the share of the secondary sector declined slightly, while that of the tertiary sector continued to rise. In 2018, the output of the tertiary sector and the secondary sector respectively accounted for 52.2 percent and 40.7 percent of China's GDP.

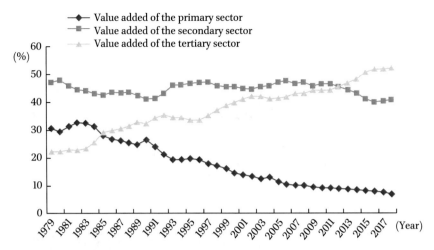

FIGURE 4.1 Composition of China's economy by sector

2.3 Characteristics of the Employment Structure and Its Changes

Industrial restructuring leads to changes in the employment structure, namely, movement of labor between sectors. As shown in Figure 4.2, the share of employment in the primary sector dropped from about seventy percent in 1979 to twenty-six percent in 2018. Since the start of reform and opening-up in China, the share of employment in China's primary sector has been declining. The changes in the employment structure do not exactly correspond to the changes in the industrial structure. The changes in China's employment structure can also be divided into three stages. The first stage is from 1978 to 1993, which saw rising shares of employment in non-agricultural sectors, i.e., the secondary and tertiary sectors. In the first stage, the primary sector, or the agricultural sector, saw a declining share in employment, but it remained the sector with the highest employment share. Meanwhile, the share of employment in the secondary sector was higher than that of the tertiary sector in this stage. In the second stage, namely from 1994 to 2010, the share of the agricultural sector employment remained the highest, while the shares of the secondary and tertiary sectors continued to rise, with the share of the tertiary sector higher than that of the secondary sector. In the third stage, namely after 2011, the tertiary sector overtook the primary sector in terms of the share in employment, and became the sector with the highest employment share. Starting from 2014, the primary sector has been the sector with the lowest employment share in China. During the thirteenth FYP period, the changes in employment across the sectors are characterized by a greater gap between the secondary and tertiary sectors in terms of employment share. In 2018, the share of employment

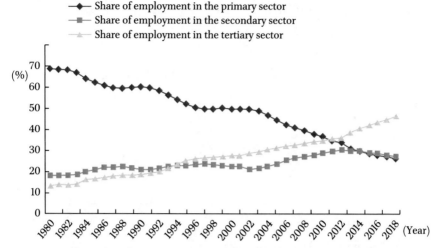

FIGURE 4.2 Share of employment in three sectors in China

in China's tertiary sector was more than forty-six percent, while that of the secondary sector was only 27.57 percent, slightly higher than that of the primary sector (26.11 percent).

2.4 *Growth Rates of the Secondary and Tertiary Sectors*

The above sections deal with the changes in industrial structure and employment structure. In this section, we will focus on the absolute growth rates of the secondary and tertiary sectors. Figure 4.3 shows the growth rates of the value added of China's secondary and tertiary sectors. As shown in Figure 4.3, before 2012, the development trend of the secondary and tertiary sectors was by and large the same. However, since 2012, the growth rate of the tertiary sector has remained higher than that of the secondary sector. During the thirteenth FYP period, the growth rate of the tertiary sector was much higher than that of the secondary sector.

2.5 *Relative Labor Productivity of the Three Sectors*

To better represent the relationship between employment structure and industrial structure, we adopted an indicator of the deviation of industrial structure and employment structure (the degree of structure deviation, i.e., the share in GDP divided by the share in employment). This indicator measures the relative labor productivity of each sector. In the absence of any asymmetry in labor productivity differences between sectors, the value of this indicator is 1 for each sector, which means that the share in employment is the same as the share in GDP. Generally, if the value of this indicator is greater than 1, it means that the share in GDP is greater than the share in employment. The greater the

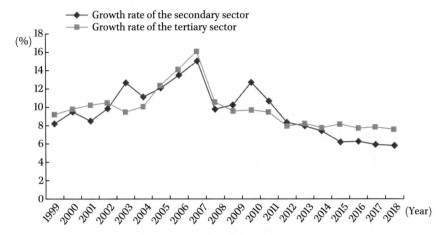

FIGURE 4.3 Growth rates of China's secondary and tertiary sectors

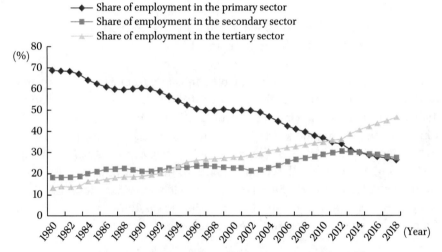

FIGURE 4.4 Degree of deviation of employment from the economy (relative labor productivity)

value, the higher the relative efficiency and labor productivity in the sector concerned. As shown in Figure 4.4, the primary sector has the lowest relative labor productivity, which keeps decreasing, and the secondary and tertiary sectors show different changes in relative labor productivity in different periods. Since the start of reform and opening-up, China's highest relative labor productivity has remained in the secondary sector. Meanwhile, the overall labor productivity of the secondary and tertiary sectors began to converge from 2004. The labor productivity gap between these two sectors was the smallest in 2016, but the divergence increased during the thirteenth FYP period.

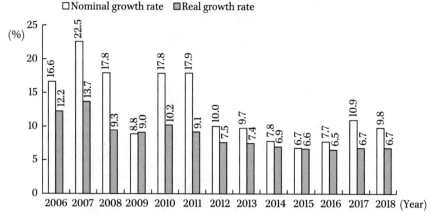

FIGURE 4.5   Growth rates of China's labor productivity

3   The Great Allocative Efficiency Resulting from Cross-Sector Industrial Restructuring Is Depleted

This section further examines the changes in China's labor productivity and how industrial restructuring affect and contribute to productivity variation amid rapid changes of the industrial structure. First, we observe the growth of China's average labor productivity, as shown in Figure 4.5. During the eleventh FYP period, the growth rate of China's labor productivity was around ten percent, except in 2009 when the country was hit by the global financial crisis. The twelfth FYP period saw a declined growth rate of labor productivity of less than ten percent, except a higher level in 2011. During the thirteenth FYP period, China's labor productivity maintained a stable growth rate.

3.1   *Labor Productivity in Three Sectors*

We calculated the labor productivity of the three sectors and the share of employment in these sectors. As shown in Table 4.1, the primary sector's productivity remains lower than that of the secondary and tertiary sectors, and the gap has been widening. Meanwhile, the share of employment in the primary sector has been decreasing, which dropped from 42.6 percent in 2006 to 26.11 percent in 2018. As a result, the movement of labor from agriculture to manufacturing and service industries in urban areas creates a great improvement in allocative efficiency. Table 4.1 also shows that the labor productivity of the tertiary sector remains lower than that of the secondary sector until 2018, while the share of employment in the tertiary sector keeps increasing. It is thus concluded that we have not seen improvement in allocative efficiency originating from within the secondary and tertiary sectors.

Using the method for calculating weighted labor productivity,[2] the labor productivity of each of the three sectors in Table 4.1 is weighted according to their respective employment share to obtain the overall labor productivity in the year concerned. As shown in Figure 4.6, the overall productivity has been on the rise, increasing from 29,300 yuan to 116,000 yuan from 2006 to 2018. To measure the contribution of industrial structure changes to overall productivity growth, further decomposition of productivity is required.

TABLE 4.1   Labor productivity of three sectors and the share of employment in three sectors

Year	Labor productivity (yuan/person)			Share in employment		
	Primary sector	Secondary sector	Tertiary sector	Primary sector	Secondary sector	Tertiary sector
2006	7,300	55,200	38,000	0.4260	0.2520	0.3220
2007	9,000	62,700	47,400	0.4080	0.2680	0.3240
2008	10,800	73,000	54,500	0.3960	0.2720	0.3320
2009	11,600	76,000	59,900	0.3810	0.2780	0.3410
2010	13,800	87,700	69,100	0.3670	0.2870	0.3460
2011	16,800	100,700	79,200	0.3480	0.2950	0.3570
2012	19,000	105,300	88,400	0.3360	0.3030	0.3610
2013	21,900	113,100	93,800	0.3140	0.3010	0.3850
2014	24,400	120,200	98,200	0.2950	0.2990	0.4060
2015	26,400	124,300	105,400	0.2830	0.2930	0.4240
2016	28,000	132,700	113,600	0.2770	0.2880	0.4350
2017	29,700	152,500	122,100	0.2698	0.2811	0.4491
2018	32,000	171,100	130,700	0.2611	0.2757	0.4632

Note: This section aims to calculate the contribution of allocative efficiency to productivity, so no price index deflator is applied in the calculation of labor productivity.
SOURCE: CALCULATION BASED ON DATA FROM *CHINA STATISTICAL YEARBOOK*

---

2 Qu Yue, "The Productivity Differences and the Losses of Allocative Efficiency of China's Industries," *The Journal of World Economy*, 12(2006).

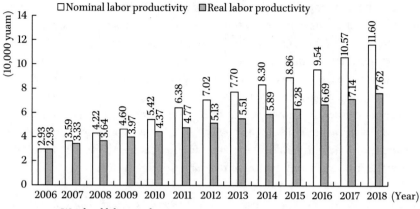

FIGURE 4.6 Weighted labor productivity

3.2 *Contribution of Allocative Efficiency Resulting from Industrial Structure Changes in the Three Sectors to Productivity Growth*

Using the method for decomposing productivity, the overall productivity is decomposed by sector into the mean value of productivity and allocative efficiency resulting from the changes in industrial structure.[3] Table 4.2 includes overall productivity b, the allocative efficiency of industrial structure a, productivity growth c and allocative efficiency improvement d. It also includes the ratio of allocative efficiency resulting from industrial structure changes to overall productivity, a/b, and the ratio of allocative efficiency improvement caused by industrial structure changes to productivity growth, d/c.

As shown in Table 4.2, the allocative efficiency from movement of labor across the three sectors, a, remains negative until it turns positive in 2013, and the allocative efficiency has been improving (d is positive). This means that cross-sector restructuring, especially between agriculture and non-agricultural sectors, leads to overall productivity growth. Currently, the sectors with higher productivity, namely the secondary and tertiary sectors, account for greater shares of employment. Meanwhile, despite the constant improvement in allocation among the three sectors, the contribution of allocation efficiency to productivity growth has started to decline after it peaked at 21.9 percent around 2014. In other words, the improvement in allocative efficiency brought about by cross-sector structural transformation and upgrade has gradually completed and started to wane. Further productivity growth needs to be

---

3 Qu Yue, "The Productivity Differences and the Losses of Allocative Efficiency of China's Industries," *The Journal of World Economy*, 12(2006).

TABLE 4.2   Contribution of allocative efficiency resulting from industrial structure changes
              in three sectors to productivity growth

Year	Allocative efficiency a	Overall productivity b	a/b	Productivity growth c	Allocative efficiency improvement d	d/c
2006	−0.4247	2.9267	−0.1451			
2007	−0.3869	3.5859	−0.1079	0.6592	0.0378	0.0573
2008	−0.3868	4.2248	−0.0915	0.6389	0.0001	0.0002
2009	−0.3191	4.5962	−0.0694	0.3713	0.0676	0.1821
2010	−0.2726	5.4151	−0.0503	0.8190	0.0465	0.0568
2011	−0.1739	6.3850	−0.0272	0.9698	0.0987	0.1018
2012	−0.0696	7.0215	−0.0099	0.6366	0.1043	0.1638
2013	0.0766	7.7031	0.0099	0.6816	0.1463	0.2146
2014	0.2076	8.3010	0.0250	0.5979	0.1310	0.2191
2015	0.3218	8.8571	0.0363	0.5561	0.1142	0.2053
2016	0.3955	9.5365	0.0415	0.6794	0.0737	0.1085
2017	0.4295	10.5713	0.0406	1.0348	0.0340	0.0329
2018	0.4799	11.6040	0.0414	1.0327	0.0504	0.0488

Note: The unit of labor productivity is 10,000 yuan/person. This section aims to calculate the
contribution of allocative efficiency to productivity, so no price index deflator is applied in
the calculation of labor productivity.
SOURCE: CALCULATION BASED ON DATA FROM *CHINA STATISTICAL YEARBOOK*

driven by the upgrade of industries towards the high end in the secondary and
tertiary sectors.

3.3   *Productivity Divergence across Industries in the Manufacturing Sector*

We also need to understand the productivity in the sub-sectors of the secondary and tertiary sectors. To this end, we can obtain the data of industrial
enterprises above designated size from the NBS, but the data of service industries are not available. Based on the data of manufacturing enterprises above
designated size from 1998 to 2012, this section examines the productivity
variation and its characteristics in labor-intensive and capital-intensive industries within the manufacturing sector. We divided industries with a two-digit

TABLE 4.3   Labor costs and (relative) productivity of different types of industries

Year	Non-labor-intensive industries	Labor-intensive industries
1998	1.035	1.000
1999	1.157	1.141
2000	1.449	1.390
2001	1.676	1.574
2002	1.920	1.758
2003	2.409	2.064
2004	3.136	2.359
2005	3.622	2.640
2006	4.365	3.074
2007	5.366	3.522
2008	6.172	3.776
2009	6.667	4.196
2012	8.820	5.299
Growth rate	7.52	4.30

Note: The labor productivity in this table is a relative indicator. The labor productivity of labor-intensive industries in 1998 is used as relative value 1. The growth rate refers to the growth rate from 1998 to 2012.
SOURCE: CALCULATED BASED ON DATA OF MANUFACTURING ENTERPRISES ABOVE DESIG-
NATED SIZES IN CHINA FROM 1998 TO 2012

industrial classification code into two groups, labor-intensive industries and non-labor-intensive industries, and calculated their labor productivity.[4]

As shown in Table 4.3, labor-intensive and non-labor-intensive industries show significant differences in labor productivity from 2000 to 2012. The divergence is shown not only in the significantly lower absolute value of labor productivity in labor-intensive industries, but also in the remarkable differences in labor productivity growth rates between the two groups. The productivity of non-labor-intensive industries is 1.7 times that of labor-intensive industries. From 1998 to 2012, the productivity of labor-intensive industries grew by 430 percent, while that of non-labor-intensive industries increased

4   Qu Yue, Cai Fang and Zhang Xiaobo, "Has the Flying Geese Paradigm Occurred in China? Analysis of China's Manufacturing Industries from 1998 to 2008," *China Economic Quarterly*, 3(2013).

by 752 percent.[5] In 2012, labor productivity divergence occurred between labor-intensive and capital-intensive industries in the manufacturing sector.

4 The Significant Contribution of Human Capital to Labor Productivity and Output

A higher level of human capital is essential for the upgrade of industrial structure in both the secondary and tertiary sectors. Therefore, an analysis of industrial upgrading and the contribution of human capital is indispensable to study of labor productivity growth. Researches on the impact of education on productivity and economic growth have only proliferated since the 1950s and 1960s, which is probably associated with the rapid economic development of the US after World War II. In China, there has also been a large number of researches on the relationship between education and economic growth in recent years.[6] A lot of empirical tests have been conducted on the impact of education on economic growth (per capita income), the findings of which are by and large consistent: investment in education has a positive effect on economic growth.

4.1 Model

In order to examine the impact of employee's human capital measured by education on the output of enterprises and how human capital plays its part, we estimated the production function to examine how the educational level of the labor force contributes to output. In the base model, while disregarding the educational level of employees, we estimated the traditional Cobb-Douglas production function which includes two factors of production, capital (k) and labor (l), and obtain the explained variable output (y) of the equation.

$$\ln y = \beta_1 \ln k + \beta_2 \ln l + \beta_3 \sum x_i + \varepsilon \quad \text{(Model 4.1)}$$

5   Qu Yue, "The Unit Labor Cost of China's Manufacturing Industries and Its Trend: A Calculation based on China's Above-scale Manufacturing Enterprises Data from 1998 to 2012," *Studies in Labor Economics*, 4(2017).

6   Lai Mingyong, Zhang Xin, Peng Shuijun, and Bao Qun, "The Source of Economic Growth: Human Capital, R&D and Technical Spillovers," *Social Sciences in China*, 2(2005); Yang Liyan, and Wang Xinli, "Human Capital, Technological Change and Endogenous Economic Growth," *China Economic Quarterly*, 4(2004); Chao Xiaojing, and Shen Kunrong, "Urban-Rural Income Disparity, Labor Quality and Economic Growth in China," *Economic Research Journal*, 6(2014).

With Model 4.1 as the base, education-related variables are added to measure human capital in various ways. Model 4.1 in Table 4.4 presents the fundamental production function obtained through an OLS estimation. According to the OLS estimation results of the production function without the education variable, the elasticity of capital and labor is about 0.382 and 0.648 respectively. That means, it is a production function with constant returns to scale.

The following methods are then used to examine how human capital (years of schooling) affects and contributes to production function. (1) Include human capital (education) as a separate input of productive factor in the Cobb Douglas production function (Model 4.2), in which the coefficient of *lnedu* is the output elasticity of education, i.e., the output growth in percentage resulting from one-percent increase in employees' average years of schooling. (2) Include human capital (education) in the Cobb Douglas production function as a multiplier of output (the contribution of which to output is similar to that of technology) (Model 4.3), in which the estimated coefficient of *edu* is the output growth in percentage resulting from each additional year of schooling of employees on average.

TABLE 4.4   Effect of years of schooling

Item	Model 4.1	Model 4.2	Model 4.3
lnk	0.382***	0.342***	0.339***
	(12.12)	(10.60)	(10.47)
lnl	0.648***	0.665***	0.667***
	(14.80)	(15.19)	(15.23)
lnedu		1.397***	
		(4.18)	
edu			0.130***
			(4.31)
_cons	1.128***	−2.038**	−0.121
	(5.77)	(−2.58)	(−0.34)
N	842	829	829
r2_a	0.567	0.577	0.577

Note: The numbers inside the brackets are t-values. *p < 0.10, **p < 0.05, ***p < 0.01. *edu* stands for years of schooling. *lnedu* stands for the logarithm of years of schooling.
SOURCE: CALCULATED BASED ON DATA FROM CHINA EMPLOYER-EMPLOYEE SURVEY (CEES) IN 2015

4.2 The Positive Effect of Years of Schooling on Output

The estimation results of Model 4.2 and Model 4.3 show respectively the output elasticity of education and the return to employees' years of schooling. According to the results, each additional year of schooling of employees is associated with a thirteen-percent increase in the output of enterprises. If years of education is considered an independent factor of production to calculate its output elasticity, on average, an increase of one percentage point in employees' years of schooling will lead to an increase of around 1.4 percentage points in output. The estimation results demonstrate that employees' educational level as a type of human capital in the production function has a significant impact on the output of enterprises. When years of schooling is included in the function, the labor elasticity increases from about 0.648 to above 0.665. Education is a special factor of production that works in combination with the labor variable. If the positive effect of education on output is ignored in production function estimation, the contribution of education tends to be attributed to other factors, resulting in underestimation of the contribution of labor and overestimation of the contribution of capital.

4.3 The Positive Effect of Different Levels of Education on Output

It is important to note that different levels of education have their distinctive characteristics. To reflect such characteristics, the labor force of different educational levels should be included in production function as a heterogeneous input of factor, resulting in a production function as follows:

$$\ln y = \beta_1 \ln k + \sum_i \beta_i \ln l_i + \beta_3 \sum x_i + \varepsilon \quad \text{(Model 4.4)}$$

l_i stands for the number of workers of different educational levels. Table 4.5 shows the models about the contribution of employees of different educational levels to output. Model 5.4 includes the number of workers of various educational levels as an independent productive factor. In order to explore the effectiveness of each educational level in contributing to output, adjacent educational levels are combined and the educational level (or combination of educational levels) that is more significant and contributes to enterprises' production is selected.

The modeling results show that as far as the output of the sample enterprises is concerned, workers with junior and senior secondary education are homogeneous, those with junior college and university education show similar characteristics, and those with secondary technical education are homogeneous with respect to both said groups. The results of Model 4.5 show that the

TABLE 4.5   Output return of a heterogeneous labor force

Item	Model 4.4	Model 4.5	Model 4.6
lnk	0.397***	0.393***	0.380***
	(15.29)	(19.36)	(18.28)
$ln(l_1)$	0.183***		
	(6.32)		
$ln(l_2)$	0.0224		
	(0.44)		
$ln(l_3)$	0.0946*		
	(1.83)		
$ln(l_4)$	0.102		
	(1.64)		
$ln(l_5)$	0.176***		
	(3.75)		
$ln(l_{12})$		0.273***	
		(9.34)	
$ln(l_{345})$		0.326***	
		(12.42)	
$ln(l_{123})$			0.299***
			(9.60)
$ln(l_{45})$			0.320***
			(11.76)
$YEAR$	YES	YES	YES
$\_cons$	2.448***	1.700***	1.837***
	(14.09)	(12.58)	(12.46)
N	1588	2242	2144
$r2\_a$	0.518	0.559	0.569

Note: The numbers inside the brackets are t-values. *$p < 0.10$, **$p < 0.05$, ***$p < 0.01$. The sub-scripts 1, 2, 3, 4 and 5 following labor (l) respectively stand for junior secondary education, senior secondary education, secondary technical education, junior college education and undergraduate education.

SOURCE: CALCULATION BASED ON DATA FROM THE CEES

elasticity of workers with junior and senior secondary education is about 0.273, and that of workers with secondary technical education and above is higher, at approximately 0.326. Model 4.6 includes workers with secondary technical education in the group with senior secondary education and below, in which the elasticity of workers with a combination of educational levels l_n (l_{123}), i.e., junior secondary education l_1, senior secondary education l_2 and secondary technical education l_3, slightly increases to 0.299, closer to the elasticity, 0.320, of workers with junior college and above education l_n (l_{45}). The results also reveal a greater return to lower levels of education including secondary technical education and below, which grows more significantly, while the output return to tertiary education including junior college education and above and its growth is not so significant.

5 Labor Productivity and Allocation of Human Capital Are Diverging, and Upgrade towards High-End Industries Is the Fundamental Path to Productivity Growth

As China presses ahead with industrial upgrading and industries in sectors start to diverge, divergence across industries is also found in allocation of human capital. With the transformation and upgrading of the country's industrial structure and its polarization, the allocation of labor force and human capital show different characteristics across industries. In order to boost productivity by improving the allocative efficiency of labor force and human capital, the characteristics of different industries should be considered in formulation of policies about industrial development and human capital accumulation.

5.1 Educational Attainment of Employees in Different Types of Industries

Enterprises are divided into labor-intensive and capital-intensive ones according to their labor intensity to examine their employee composition in terms of educational attainment and the quantity of simple labor. As shown in Figure 4.7, the educational attainment of employees of labor-intensive enterprises concentrates in the lower-level range with an average number of years of schooling being about ten years (corresponding to approximately junior secondary education); the employees of capital-intensive enterprises include both high-skilled and low-skilled workers, and there are two peaks in the distribution of years of schooling, i.e., ten years and thirteen years, respectively corresponding to junior secondary education and junior college education.

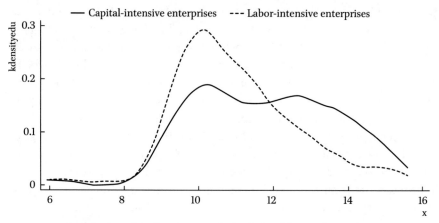

FIGURE 4.7 Distribution of employee's years of schooling in labor- and capital-intensive
enterprises in 2015

5.2   *Allocation of Human Capital by Industry*

Corresponding to their access to human capital, simple labor input productivity and education productivity are both higher in capital-intensive industries. The allocative efficiency of education is largely positive and keeps increasing in both labor-intensive and capital-intensive enterprises. The allocation of simple labor input, however, is the opposite in these two types of enterprises with different capital intensity: the allocation of simple labor is negative in capital-intensive enterprises, while in labor-intensive enterprises, it is positive and shows an upward trend.

TABLE 4.6   Allocation of human capital in labor-intensive and capital-intensive industries

Year	Simple labor input					
	Capital-intensive industries			Labor-intensive industries		
	2013	2014	2015	2013	2014	2015
Allocation a	−5.208	−8.084	−9.644	0.384	0.628	0.779
Weighted productivity b	14.161	16.623	17.625	5.408	6.212	7.656

TABLE 4.6   Allocation of human capital (*cont.*)

Year	Education					
	Capital-intensive industries			Labor-intensive industries		
	2013	2014	2015	2013	2014	2015
Allocation a	62.161	65.388	101.748	−2.825	4.220	11.535
Weighted productivity b	1414.0	1536.4	1684.0	563.6	606.0	815.2

Unit: 10,000 yuan/person
SOURCE: CALCULATION BASED ON DATA FROM THE CEES

The above calculation and analysis show that labor-intensive industries are now along a well-trodden path to development after years of development. Meanwhile, China has also determined its objective of industrial upgrading as high-end capital-intensive industries. These industries have higher simple labor input productivity and education productivity, but their allocation of human capital is complicated. Enterprises that have made it to higher-end industries are facing enormous challenges. Whether they can successfully transform themselves into high-end innovative enterprises depends on their ability to make use of skilled workers to pursue innovation-driven development and improve their allocation of human capital.

6   Conclusions and Policy Implications

Thanks to the transfer of surplus rural labor to modern urban sectors and the rapid increase in the share of urban secondary and tertiary sectors, China has seen a significant increase in labor productivity resulting from reallocation across the three sectors. As China becomes a middle-income country and the absolute number of its working-age population starts to decrease, the country is in urgent need of further industrial upgrading and productivity improvement, especially development towards the high end in the secondary and tertiary sectors, to drive its further economic development. This cannot be achieved without improvement in human capital. In an era when the human capital level in China is rising rapidly and its contribution to economic growth is becoming increasingly important, it is vital to fully understand the contribution of different components of human capital to productivity and economic growth. With the transformation and upgrade of China's industrial structure and its polarization, the productivity and allocation of labor and human capital thereof have shown disparate characteristics in different industries. Considering that China's initial rapid economic growth has been driven by its labor-intensive industries, it is important to maintain a balance between industrial transformation and upgrading and a steady progress in traditional labor-intensive industries with an accumulation of human capital. To be specific, emerging industries should play a major role in industrial upgrading, shifting to new growth drivers, and productivity improvement, and traditional industries should ensure a smooth transition during the economic transformation by laying a solid foundation for economic development and creating jobs. In the context of further industrial transformation and upgrading and labor productivity divergence, in order to boost productivity by improving the allocative efficiency of labor and human capital, the design of policies about human capital accumulation and industrial development should take into account the characteristics of human capital allocation at various levels and the development paths of different industries.

CHAPTER 5

Increase in Local Employment and Job Polarization among Migrants

*Yang Ge**

Over the past three decades, China has seen migration of people from rural to urban areas on a scale unprecedented in the history of mankind amid its rapid economic growth, industrialization and urbanization.

The migrant population in China has been expanding rapidly. According to the population census in 1982, there were 6.57 million migrants in China in 1982. The figure more than tripled to 21.35 million in 1990. The fastest growth of migrants in China was seen from 1990 to 2000. In 2000, the number of migrants in China exceeded 100 million, which was nearly five times the number in 1990. After that period, although the growth of migrants slowed down slightly, the growth rate has remained high. The number of migrants in China reached 220 million in 2010 and a record-high of 253 million in 2014. However, since the start of the thirteenth FYP period, the migrant population in China has been decreasing, the number of which dropped to 241 million in 2018.

Changes occurred to China's social and economic development during the thirteenth FYP period. First, new urbanization, household registration reform and related social institutions were elevated to an unprecedented strategic level. The government made comprehensive plans for future urban systems and the reform of household registration system, which will definitely have a profound impact on the future distribution of population in various regions. Second, China's economy shifted from ultra-high-speed growth to steady medium-to-high-speed growth, and its economic development pattern has been completely transformed. Third, in the southeast coastal regions, major progress was made in industrial upgrading, and industrial restructuring and industrial relocation were both well under way. The combined effects of these changes have led to new trends and characteristics in China's migrants.

What social and economic factors will affect China's migrants in the fourteenth FYP period? Currently, the international division of labor is changing, and the risks of trade conflict are accumulating. China will stick to supply-side

* Yang Ge is an associate professor at the Institute of Population and Labor Economics, CASS, and his research interests are population mobility and development.

structural reform to upgrade its industrial structure. It will constantly adjust its population and birth policies, accelerating the household registration reform, and deepen the reform of its social and economic systems. The transformation in areas such as population, economy and society in China is causing a transformation of population migration and mobility.

The following sections analyze the employment trends of migrants in China during the fourteenth FYP period based on data from population censuses, population sample surveys and the CMDS. In China, the definition of migrants is based on household registration. Accordingly, migrants in China refer to people who migrate across townships and subdistricts, counties, districts and provinces, who are working, doing business or living in places other than their household registration areas.

1 Migration Changes

1.1 *Shrinking Size of China's Migrant Population*

Although China's migrant population has been growing rapidly over the past thirty years, its growth rate has been declining in recent years. The annual growth rate of migrants in China, which was 7.57 percent from 2000 to 2005 and 8.49 percent from 2005 to 2010, dropped to 2.21 percent from 2010 to 2015. Population migration in China saw a turning point at the beginning of the thirteenth FYP period primarily due to demographic, economic and policy factors. According to the "Communique on One-percent National Population Sample Survey in 2015", the number of people who live in places other than their household registration areas stood at 294 million. That included 247 million

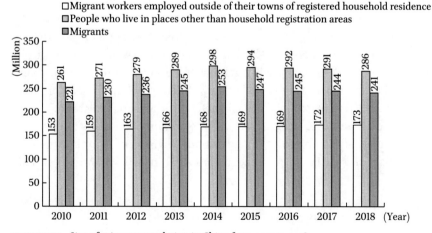

FIGURE 5.1   Size of migrant population in China from 2010 to 2018

migrants, a decrease of nearly six million from 2014. It is the first time since the start of reform and opening-up in China that the size of migrant population has decreased. During the thirteenth FYP period, the size of China's migrant population kept declining, with an annual decrease of three million.

Negative growth in the number of migrants is also found in big cities such as Beijing and Shanghai. After dramatic population expansion from 2000 to 2009, Shanghai and Beijing both saw significant slowdown in growth of permanent and migrant population after 2010, and their migrant population began to decrease in 2015 and 2016. According to Shanghai Municipal Bureau of Statistics, at the end of 2015, the permanent population of Shanghai stood at 24,152,700, a decrease of 104,100 from 2014, including 9,816,500 permanent migrants, down by 147,700. In Beijing, the number of permanent migrants was 8,226,000 in 2015, which dropped to 8,075,000 in 2016. The population in downtown Beijing also registered a negative growth in 2016.

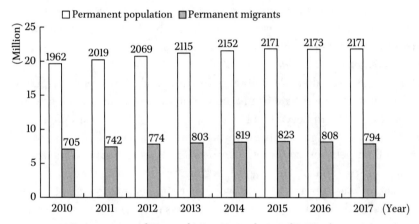

FIGURE 5.2 Permanent population and migrant population of Beijing from 2010 to 2017

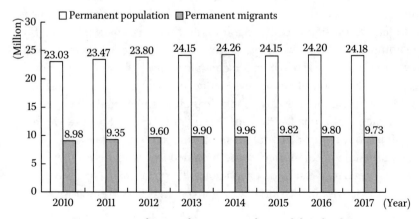

FIGURE 5.3 Permanent population and migrant population of Shanghai from 2010 to 2017

The negative population growth in Beijing and Shanghai is closely associated with China's urbanization strategy. The "New Urbanization Plan (2014–2020)" of the country prescribes the basic principle of "strictly controlling the population size of megacities with a population of more than five million in downtown areas". Following the central governments' policies, the governments of megacities have introduced population control targets at various levels. Local governments' strict population control measures have inhibited population mobility, resulting in the reduced size of migrant population or a slowdown in migrants' growth rate in first-tier Chinese cities. Therefore, the trends of migrants in Beijing and Shanghai are not universal. Nonetheless, the migrant population in China is experiencing a transition from high-speed growth to low-speed growth. Such transition is primarily caused by demographic and economic changes, such as the economic new normal with declining economic growth rate and a shrinking working-age population. In view of the aforesaid, is it true that China's migrant population has started declining?

In addition to population census and population sample surveys, the annual monitoring survey of migrant workers conducted by the NBS also serves as a source of data for calculating migrants in China. According to the *Migrant Workers Monitoring Survey Report 2018*, the total number of migrant workers in China in 2018 stood at 288 million, an increase of 0.6 percent compared with 2017, and its growth rate from 2016 to 2017 was 1.7 percent. The growth of migrant workers employed outside the towns of registered household residence also declined significantly, with the annual increase falling from close to four million between 2010 and 2014 to one million after 2014. The size of migrant workers is still expanding, but its growth rate is obviously declining.

The data of migrants and migrant workers in the said surveys are obtained are obtained in different ways. The NBS estimates the size of China's migrant population based on data from population sample surveys, including population censuses, one-percent population sample surveys (such as those conducted in 2005 and 2015) and one-per-thousand population sample surveys, which are all conducted in migration destinations. The NBS' estimation of the number of migrant workers in China is based on data from monitoring surveys of migrant workers which are conducted on the basis of rural household surveys. Rural household surveys contain employment data of rural labor force. It is supplemented by household migration survey and other specific surveys, which are conducted in places of migrants' origin. Some researchers have pointed out that for two reasons, migrant statistics obtained in places of origin are more accurate than those obtained in destinations. First, some migrants do not have a stable job or residence. They may often change employers and addresses, live in the workplace, or do not have a fixed employer, which makes it difficult for interviewers comprising primarily grassroots staff to collect data about all migrants. Second, surveys in places of origin have access to migrants' household registration information, so they can easily figure out the number of people concerned even in cases of household migration.

Therefore, data from the monitoring surveys of migrant workers probably reflect more accurate trends of population migration: the migrant population in China has shifted from high-speed growth to low-speed growth, and even from growth to negative growth. The changes in the size of migrants in China are mainly caused by factors in three areas, namely population, economic development, and policies and reform.

First, demographic factors are the root cause of the falling growth rate of migrants in China. China's working-age population aged fifteen to sixty-four and its proportion in the country's total population have been declining since 2013 and 2010 respectively. In the meanwhile, the new entrants to rural labor force has decreased significantly, and the scale and speed of rural labor migration have also dropped significantly. Duan (2019) claimed that the number of young adults with rural household registration would decline by age cohort in 2020: the number of people aged twenty to twenty-two would be 2.72 million less than that of people aged twenty-three to twenty-five, and the number of people aged twenty-two to twenty-four would be 3.14 million less than that of people aged twenty-five to twenty-seven. In the long run, the total fertility rate in China and the fertility rate of Chinese women in rural areas will keep declining. Consequently, the current trends of age structure of the Chinese population will remain unchanged in a long period of time.

Second, economic factors are the second leading cause of changes in China's migrant population. Although China's economy has maintained a medium-to-high growth rate over the past five years, compared with ten to twenty years ago, significant changes have taken place in China's economy, including a transition from the inefficient ultra-high-speed growth to stable high-quality growth, a decline of GDP growth rate from ten percent to six to seven percent, and a thorough transformation of the industrial structure. Since 2015, the value added of the service sector has accounted for half of the country's GDP, and it has been growing faster than that of the agricultural and industrial sectors. Traditional labor-intensive industries absorb a large number of migrant workers, in which two major changes are taking place. First, humans are being replaced by intelligent robots. Second, these industries are moving to regions with lower labor costs, such as China's central and western regions and Southeast Asian countries. The supply-side structural reform in China focusing on cutting overcapacity, reducing excess inventory, deleveraging, lowering costs, and strengthening areas of weakness has been making progress. Energy-intensive and highly polluting industries are being upgraded and restructured. All these economic factors have an impact on population migration and mobility.

Third, China's household registration policies are also an important cause of the declining growth of migrants in the country. Since the start of the thirteenth FYP period, China has been pressing forward with its household registration reform. According to the "Opinions on Further Advancing the Reform of Household Registration System" issued by the State Council, by 2020, 100 million people of rural household registration and other types of long-term residents already living in cities and towns will be granted urban household registration status by cities and towns of various levels by 2020. Accordingly, many large cities have relaxed their household registration requirements, some small and medium-sized cities have lifted restrictions in this regard, and mega-cities have introduced point-based household registration systems and other measures to grant local household registration to migrants with stable jobs and residences. As a result, some eligible migrants and their families have obtained household registration in the places where they live, and are no longer migrants.

1.2   *Changing Characteristics of Migration in China*

First, the proportion of short-distance, intra-provincial migration is increasing.

Calculation based on census data shows that the proportion of inter-provincial migrants in China's migrant population has been declining since it increased from 26.1 percent in 1990 to 46.1 percent in 2005, which dropped to 39.4 percent in 2015, while that of intra-provincial migrants has been on the rise in the past decade.[1]

The monitoring surveys of migrant workers conducted by the NBS of China reveal similar characteristics in the migration distance of migrant workers employed outside their towns of registered household residence. Long-distance inter-provincial migration dominated the migration in China before 2010. The proportion of inter-provincial migrants in China's migrant population reached 50.3 percent in 2010. But the figure has been falling, and dropped to forty-four percent in 2018.

Second, China's central and western regions are replacing the east as the central migration destinations.

China has seen remarkable progress in industrial upgrading in its southeastern coastal provinces, and labor-intensive industries in the country have been

---

1   Duan Chengrong, Xie Donghong, and Lyu Lidan, "Migration Transition in China," *Population Research*, 2(2019), 12–20.

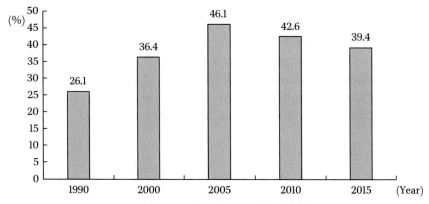

FIGURE 5.4 Proportion of inter-provincial migrants in China's migrant population

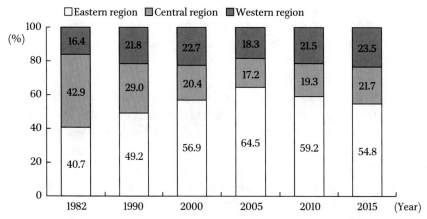

FIGURE 5.5 Proportion of migrants with China's eastern, central and western regions as destinations in the migrant population

relocated to the central and western regions, causing a transition in the flow of migrants. The migrants in the central and western regions are growing significantly faster than in the eastern region, and the proportions of migrants in the central and western regions have been increasing. As shown in Figure 5.5, from 2005 to 2015, the proportion of migrants in the eastern region dropped from 64.5 percent to 54.8 percent, while that of migrants in the central and western regions increased respectively from 17.2 percent to 21.7 percent, and from 18.3 percent to 23.5 percent.

According to the monitoring surveys of migrant workers conducted by the NBS, from 2010 to 2018, the number of migrant workers employed in the country's eastern region dropped from 162 million to 158 million, and the proportion of these migrant workers in the total dropped from 66.9 percent to 54.8 percent.

Meanwhile, migrant workers employed in the central and western regions increased in terms of both size and share in the total. In 2018, migrant workers employed in the Yangtze River Delta and the Pearl River Delta respectively accounted for 18.9 percent and 15.7 percent of the total, down by approximately five percentage points from 24.0 percent and 20.9 percent in 2010. The proportion of migrant workers employed in central and western regions, on the other hand, increased from 32.8 percent in 2010 to 41.8 percent in 2018.

2 Characteristics and Changes of Migrants' Employment

2.1 *Ageing of Migrants*
An important characteristic of migrants in China is the dominance of young working-age population. Nonetheless, China's migrants are ageing. Due to age selectivity of population migration, migrants have the lowest dependency ratio in the total population. In China, working-age population account for eighty percent of the total migrant population. The working-age migrants, however, are clearly ageing. According to population census data,[2] from 1982 to 2015, the average age and median age of China's migrants increased respectively from twenty-eight years and twenty-three years to thirty-one years. The CMDS data show that, from 2010 to 2017, the average age of migrants in China rose from 27.83 years to 30.21 years, the median age increased from twenty-nine years to thirty-one years, and the proportion of migrants aged forty-five and above in the total migrant population increased from 9.0 percent to 19.6 percent (see Table 5.1). The ageing of the migrant labor force makes economic transformation an increasingly pressing task for China.

Migrant workers in China are also ageing. According to the monitoring surveys of migrant workers conducted by the NBS, the average age of migrant workers employed in and outside their towns of registered household residence increased from thirty-six years and thirty-one years in 2020 to 44.9 years and 35.2 years in 2018 respectively. A lot of migrant workers in their fifties are still working. The proportion of people aged fifty and above in China's migrant workers employed in and outside their towns of registered household residence rose from 24.1 percent and 4.7 percent in 2010 to 33.2 percent and 11.1 percent in 2018 respectively.

---

2 Duan Chengrong, Xie Donghong, and Lyu Lidan, "Migration Transition in China," *Population Research*, 2(2019), 12–20.

TABLE 5.1   Age composition of China's migrants in 2010 and 2017

	Age (years)	2017	2010
Age composition (%)	0~14	21.1	18.5
	15~4	10.9	17.5
	25~34	27.1	29.8
	35~44	21.3	25.2
	45~54	14.0	7.3
	55~64	3.9	1.4
	65 and above	1.7	0.3
Average age (years)		30.21	27.83
Median age (years)		31	29

SOURCE: CALCULATION BASED ON DATA FROM THE CMDS IN 2010 AND 2017

2.2   *Improved Educational Attainment of Migrants*

On average, the educational attainment of migrants in China has been increasing rapidly. According to population census data,[3] the average years of schooling of China's migrants was 5.6 years in 1982, slightly higher than the average of 5.5 years of the total population. It increased to 10.6 years in 2015, much higher than the average of 9.1 years of the total population.

This conclusion is also supported by data from other sources. According to data from the CMDS, from 2010 to 2017, the proportion of migrants with junior secondary education and below dropped significantly, while the proportion of migrants with senior secondary education increased from 19.7 percent to 22.0 percent, and that of migrants with junior college education and above increased by a wide margin from 7.5 percent to 17.0 percent (see Figure 5.7). The CMDS data also show that the average years of schooling of China's migrants increased from 9.36 years in 2010 to 10.10 years in 2017.

The monitoring survey of migrant workers conducted by the NBS also reflects the improved quality of human resources of migrant workers. In 2018, more than half of the migrant workers in China were born in the 1980s. As people born in the 1980s and 1990s account for an increasing proportion of China's migrant workers, the educational attainment of migrant workers in general has been increasing. Moreover, migrant workers are not only employed in

---

3   Duan Chengrong, Xie Donghong, and Lyu Lidan, "Migration Transition in China," *Population Research*, 2(2019), 12–20.

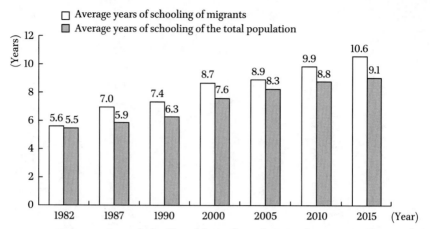

FIGURE 5.6   Average years of schooling of the total population and migrants in China aged
             six and above

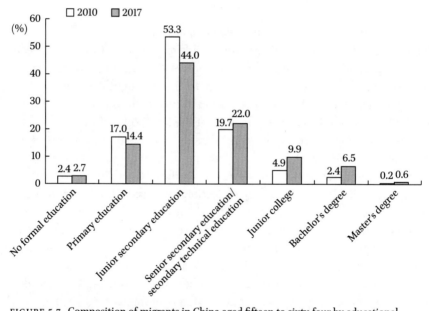

FIGURE 5.7   Composition of migrants in China aged fifteen to sixty-four by educational
             attainment in 2010 and 2017

low-skilled jobs that are generally considered dirty, tiring and arduous. In 2018, the proportion of migrant workers with junior college education and above continued to rise, respectively accounting for 13.8 percent and 8.1 percent of migrant workers employed in and outside their towns of registered household residence, up from 7.0 percent and 3.4 percent in 2011.

2.3   *Better Jobs of Migrants*

Thanks to the improved quality of human capital, migrants' jobs are significantly improved. Besides assembly line workers, construction workers and vendors, the migrant population also include high-income gold-collar workers, successful entrepreneurs, and high-skilled professionals. Data from the CMDS can shed some light in this regard, so the data of seven megacities, i.e., Beijing, Shanghai, Guangzhou, Shenzhen, Tianjin, Wuhan, and Chongqing, are used for analysis. These cities include first-tier cities and central cities in China's central and western regions, a study of which can reveal the changes in migrants' jobs in China. As shown in Table 5.2, there was a significant rise in the proportion of technicians in China's migrant population in Beijing, Shanghai, Tianjin and Guangzhou from 2010 to 2017.

TABLE 5.2   Composition of migrants in China's megacities by occupation in 2010 and 2017

City	Year	Head of state departments, Party organizations, civil organizations, businesses, public institutions (%)	Technicians (%)	Civil servants, clerks, and related workers (%)	Workers in commerce and services sector (%)	Workers in agriculture, forestry, animal husbandry, fishery, water conservation (%)	Operators of manufacturing and transport facilities and related workers (%)	No stable job (%)
Beijing	2010	2.64	16.00	9.94	61.05	2.06	5.79	2.54
	2017	1.13	20.25	3.12	60.67	1.22	8.77	0.93
Tianjin	2010	1.32	6.97	3.77	40.43	2.36	31.1	14.04
	2017	0.29	9.23	0.82	58.33	1.23	25.42	1.87
Shanghai	2010	3.46	10.93	9.77	35.19	0.69	36.94	3.02
	2017	0.91	17.23	2.69	45.61	1.5	27.01	1.23
Guangzhou	2010	2.09	9.86	7.19	37.24	1.97	38.11	3.54
	2017	0.40	13.3	1.45	62.54	0.1	17.02	0.67
Wuhan	2010	1.53	4.73	3.34	80.67	0.42	5.42	3.89
	2017	0.47	5.50	0.82	77.17	2.58	9.48	1.41
Shenzhen	2010	3.49	13.32	14.63	39.86	0.74	24.72	3.24
	2017	0.68	14.56	1.84	48.19	0.07	26.75	1.53
Chongqing	2010	2.5	11.01	10.36	55.47	0.07	16.08	4.5
	2017	0.77	10.45	3.71	57.21	0.59	21.89	2.8

SOURCE: CALCULATED BASED ON THE CMDS IN 2010 AND 2017

2.4   *Steadily Increasing Income of Migrants*

The income of China's migrants has maintained a high growth rate. According to data from the CMDS (see Table 5.3), the mean monthly income of China's migrants more than doubled from 2010 to 2017, with an average annual growth rate of 12.8 percent, higher than that of the country's GDP and national income during the same period. The median monthly income of China's migrants increased from 1,500 yuan in 2010 to 4,000 yuan in 2017. The share of high-income migrants has also increased. In 2010, migrants earning more than 5000 yuan per month accounted for about 5.5 percent of China's total migrant population. In 2017, 7.4 percent of China's migrants have a monthly income of more than 10,000 yuan.

The income of migrants in China's megacities has also grown remarkably (see Table 5.4). From 2010 to 2017, the income growth of migrants in Beijing and Tianjin exceeded the average income growth of China's migrant population. During this period, the mean monthly income of migrants in the selected cities except Wuhan rose at an annual growth rate of more than ten percent. In terms of the mean monthly income in 2017, migrants in Shanghai ranked first, followed by those in Beijing and Shenzhen with roughly the same monthly income, and migrants in Wuhan and Guangzhou ranked fourth and fifth. Among the megacities in question, Chongqing had the lowest mean monthly income of migrants.

TABLE 5.3   Composition of China's migrants by income and migrants' mean and median monthly income in 2010 and 2017

Item	2010	2017
Below 1000 (%)	6.02	0.98
1000~1999 (%)	50.75	5.26
2000~2999 (%)	25.97	16.23
3000~4999 (%)	11.81	42.20
5000~7999 (%)	3.61	23.22
8000~9999 (%)	0.60	4.65
10000~19999 (%)	0.69	5.36
20000 and above (%)	0.55	2.09
Mean monthly income (yuan)	2123.96	4936.21
Median monthly income(yuan)	1500.00	4000.00

SOURCE: CALCULATION BASED ON THE CMDS IN 2010 AND 2017

TABLE 5.4   Income of migrants in China's megacities in 2010 and 2017

Megacity	2017		2010		Annual growth rate (%)
	Mean	Median	Mean	Median	
Beijing	6638.88	5000	2683.98	2000	13.81
Tianjin	4390.66	3500	1805.65	1500	13.53
Shanghai	6834.23	5000	2925.42	2000	12.89
Guangzhou	4926.34	4000	2450.87	1750	10.49
Wuhan	5023.80	4000	3489.91	1500	5.34
Shenzhen	6616.11	5000	3076.50	2000	11.56
Chongqing	3970.88	3191	1795.74	1500	12.00

Unit: Yuan
SOURCE: CALCULATION BASED ON THE CMDS IN 2010 AND 2017

2.5   Migrants Moving towards the High End of the Industrial Chain for Jobs

As China makes steady progress in industrial upgrading, the industries in which migrants seek jobs are also changing, with them moving towards the high end of the industrial chain in employment. Nationally, from 2010 to 2017, the industries with the highest share of migrants in China remained manufacturing, wholesale and retail, residential services, repair and other services, accommodation and catering, and construction, each with a share of more than five percent. More than eighty percent of China's migrants are employed in these industries. The share of each of the aforementioned industries in migrants' employment, however, has slightly dropped, while that of education, finance, information transmission, software and information technology services has increased. The change suggests that China's migrants are moving towards the high end of the industrial chain for jobs, though they have a long way to go.

As shown in Table 5.6, big changes have also taken place in megacities in the industries in which migrants seek jobs, reflecting the following characteristics. First, the manufacturing industry is being relocated to China's central and western regions. The share of Guangzhou's migrants employed in the manufacturing industry dropped from 46.5 percent in 2010 to 33.3 percent in 2017. In Wuhan and Chongqing, the share of migrants working in the manufacturing industry rose respectively from 7.7 percent and 15.5 percent in 2010 to 17.9 percent and 24.9 percent in 2017. Second, the population deconcentration policies

TABLE 5.5   Composition of China's migrants' income in megacities in 2010 and 2017

Rank	2010 (%)		2017 (%)	
1	Manufacturing	40.38	Manufacturing	38.57
2	Wholesale and retail	17.70	Wholesale and retail	17.90
3	Social services	10.79	Accommodation and catering	9.88
4	Accommodation and catering	10.27	Residential services, repair, and other services	9.25
5	Construction	6.21	Construction	6.81
6	Transport, storage, postal services, and communications	4.09	Transport, storage, and postal services	3.53
7	Miscellaneous	2.97	Real estate	2.32
8	Scientific research and technological services	2.43	Education	2.08
9	Education, culture, sports, broadcasting, film and television	1.14	Health and social work	1.96
10	Agriculture, forestry, husbandry, and fishery	1.11	Information transmission, software, and information technology services	1.66
11	Finance, insurance, and real estate	1.06	Finance	1.30
12	Health, sports, and public welfare	0.82	Agriculture, forestry, husbandry, and fishery	1.16
13	Production and supply of electricity, coal and water	0.44	Culture, sports, and entertainment	0.95
14	Mining	0.31	Public administration, social security, and civil organizations	0.69
15	Party and state agencies, civil organizations	0.29	Leasing and commercial services	0.50
16			Mining	0.41
17			Water conservancy, environmental protection, and public utility management	0.36
18			Production and supply of electricity, heat, gas and water	0.35

TABLE 5.5 Composition of China's migrants' income in megacities in 2010 and 2017 (*cont.*)

Rank	2010 (%)		2017 (%)	
19			Scientific research and technological services	0.33
20			International organizations	0.01
	Primary sector	1.11		1.16
	Secondary sector	47.34		46.14
	Tertiary sector	51.55		52.71
	Sum	100.0	Sum	100.0

SOURCE: CALCULATED BASED ON THE CMDS IN 2010 AND 2017

TABLE 5.6 Composition of migrants in China's megacities by industry in 2010 and 2017

City	Year	Primary sector	Secondary sector	Tertiary sector	Manufacturing	Construction	Wholesale and retail	Accommodation and catering	Residential services, repair and other services	Finance and real estate
Beijing	2010	1.2	14.6	84.2	7.7	6.5	30.1	17.2	17.2	1.7
	2017	1.2	29.5	69.4	21.1	7.7	17.6	9.6	14.8	5.3
Tianjin	2010	0.4	37.4	62.2	29.4	7.3	12.7	14.6	14.9	1.0
	2017	1.5	41.1	57.4	35.1	5.6	19.3	11.9	12.6	2.6
Shanghai	2010	0.9	49.7	49.4	39.1	10.3	16.9	9.4	9.9	1.3
	2017	1.8	47.4	50.8	39.0	8.2	13.9	6.6	8.6	5.0
Guangzhou	2010	1.7	51.6	46.7	46.5	4.2	20.0	7.9	6.9	1.0
	2017	0.0	37.2	62.8	33.3	3.6	23.4	10.0	9.3	4.3
Wuhan	2010	0.4	9.5	90.1	7.7	1.4	45.8	13.9	19.5	0.4
	2017	2.9	24.7	72.4	17.9	6.5	30.4	13.3	14.4	3.6
Shenzhen	2010	0.7	38.0	61.3	34.4	2.7	18.7	7.6	14.0	2.9
	2017	0.1	48.1	51.9	44.4	3.5	16.5	6.3	7.0	4.9
Chongqing	2010	0.1	26.1	73.8	15.5	8.6	22.5	12.6	19.2	2.6
	2017	1.2	36.1	62.7	24.9	10.4	18.7	10.6	12.0	6.0

SOURCE: CALCULATION BASED ON THE CMDS IN 2010 AND 2017

of some megacities have proved effective. In Beijing, for example, the proportion of migrants working in traditional service industries, such as wholesale and retail, accommodation and catering, residential services, repair and other services, declines significantly, while the proportion of migrants employed in finance, real estate and other new types of service industries increases considerably. The same change is also observed in Shanghai and Shenzhen.

3   An Analysis of Migrants' Employment Trends in the Fourteenth FYP Period

In summary, China's migrant population has shown the following changes. First, due to changes in the age structure of the population, the migration of rural labor force to other sectors for employment is slowing down, and the growth rate of China's migrants is steadily declining, which has turned negative. Second, migration for employment is shifting from large-scale inter-provincial mobility to intra-city and intra-province migration for jobs, and cities in China's central and western regions have become migration destinations. Third, the ageing trend of migrants continues. Fourth, the steadily improving educational attainment of migrants in general enables them better jobs and considerably improved income. Fifth, migrants are employed in an increasing variety of industries, and the proportion of technicians in the total migrant population is increasing.

The demographic, economic and policy environments for China during the fourteenth FYP period will not only maintain the characteristics during the previous FYP period, but will also show new characteristics. The rising risk of international trade conflicts may accelerate industrial restructuring and relocation, which will have a negative impact on migrants working in some industries and cause them greater unemployment risks. China will continue to focus on the supply-side structural reform to promote industrial upgrading, and will vigorously support the development of technological and innovative industries, which will create new jobs and reduce unemployment. Meanwhile, the continued adjustment to birth policies still cannot reverse the population ageing trend, and the number of new migrant workers will keep decreasing. A new round of household registration reform will be launched, the reform of land, education, social security and other related policies will significantly reduce the restrictions on mobility, and the number of migrants obtaining household registration in places where they work will increase significantly. How will these economic, demographic and policy changes affect migrants' employment?

First, the ageing of the migrant population and new job expectations of new generation of migrants will cause a labor shortage in some industries. New generation of migrants and older ones show considerable differences in their employment expectations, because young people expect better working environment, life and entertainment, and greater room for career advancement. As a result, some industries will be short of workers. This is especially true for the construction industry. With an apparently ageing workforce, the construction industry does not appeal to young people even with high salaries. Township and village enterprises, which used to be a synonym for China's vibrant private economy and play an important role in some regions' economic development, are also confronted with an ageing workforce and difficulty recruiting workers. Preferring big cities with better development prospects and more life and entertainment options, young people show little interest in working for local township and village enterprises.

Second, the improved human capital quality of migrant workers will be a catalyst for industrial upgrading. Currently, China's industrial structure is undergoing a gradual transition from the dominance of labor-intensive, resource-processing, and heavy and chemical industries to a leading role of capital-, technology- and knowledge-intensive industries. In 2018, the tertiary sector accounted for 52.2 percent of China's GDP, far exceeding the share of the secondary sector. In the secondary sector, the proportion of traditional industries, especially energy-intensive industries and the mining industry using energy as raw material, has been gradually decreasing, while that of equipment manufacturing and high-tech manufacturing industries has been increasing. Emerging industries, including industrial robots, optoelectronic devices, new energy vehicles, have been growing fast. The development of new industries, new products and new business forms and the migrants' quality improvement will boost each other and form a virtuous cycle. The proportion of high-quality migrants has been increasing. According to census data, the proportion of migrants with an educational attainment at junior college level and above rose from 4.8 percent in 2000 to 23.2 percent in 2015.

Third, the increase in migrants seeking local jobs in their home provinces will promote the development of central cities and city clusters in China's central and western regions. The regional distribution of China's migrant population is changing. In the past decade, the proportions of intra-provincial migrants and migrants with China's central and western regions as destinations have been rising. This reflects the increasing appeal of central and western cities to China's migrants. Many central cities in China's central and western regions, such as Wuhan, Chengdu, Zhengzhou and so on, have become megacities with a population of more than ten million people one after another. In future, the

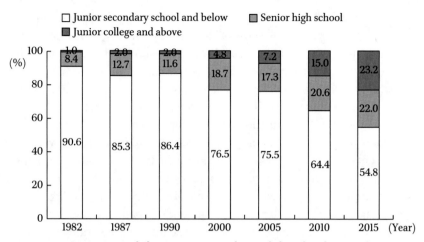

FIGURE 5.8 Composition of China's migrants aged six and above by educational
attainment

city clusters in China's central and western regions will emerge as new economic growth poles of the country, and they will play an increasingly important role in the development of industrial clusters and attracting population.

Fourth, industrial restructuring will lead to further job polarization among migrants. China's accelerated industrial restructuring will lead to polarization in migrants' employment in two ways, which can be summarized as the coexistence of shortage and surplus, and the coexistence of improvement and difficulty. First, polarization is shown in the coexistence of labor shortage and labor surplus. On the one hand, the development of emerging industries creates a huge demand for relevant workers. There will be short-term labor shortage in such industries, including new residential service industries such as health service, cultural and creative service, tourism, and education, and producer services such as R&D and design, modern supply chain, science and technology, finance, testing and inspection, and branding. On the other hand, as traditional industries, especially energy-intensive and highly polluting ones such as coal, cement, iron and steel, and chemical industries, relocate or cease operation, migrants working in these industries are facing greater unemployment risks. Second, polarization is shown in the coexistence of rapidly growing number of high-income migrants and the difficulty increasing income for some groups of migrants. In China, the number of migrants earning more than 10,000 yuan per month has been increasing, but migrant workers face greater unemployment risks. Migrant workers tend to be hit by industrial restructuring, and it is difficult for them to find better jobs. According to the monitoring surveys of migrant workers of the NBS, migrant workers in China are moving from the secondary sector to the tertiary sector for jobs. In 2010, the manufacturing industry absorbed the most migrant workers, accounting for 36.7 percent of the total, but the figure dropped to 27.9 percent in 2018. The share of migrant workers in the tertiary sector, on the other hand, has been increasing. In 2018, more than fifty percent of China's migrant workers are employed in the tertiary sector, mainly in traditional service industries, such as accommodation and catering, residential services, repair and other services. Low-skilled migrants with a low level of educational attainment are the most vulnerable to unemployment and income stagnation.

4 Policy Recommendations

The migration changes in China are caused by several factors including migrants' demographic changes, industrial structure and distribution of industries. In the four decades since the start of reform and opening-up in China, the migrant population made a great contribution to the country's economic development. Facing the new trends of migration in the new era, the following efforts should be made to promote innovation in all areas of social and economic systems.

First, deepen the household registration reform to establish a new system in this regard. China's household registration reform is now on the fast track. Currently, the household registration reform mainly consists of efforts in three aspects. First, establish an urban-rural unified household registration system and eliminate the differences between agricultural and non-agricultural household registration. Second, implement a residence permit system in big cities, and give permit holders the same treatment as residents with local household registration. Third, lift household registration restrictions on migrants in small and medium-sized cities, and relax the restrictions in big cities except for a few megacities. The National Development and Reform Commission (NDRC) of China issued the "Guidelines on Fostering and Developing Modern Metropolitan Areas" in March 2019, which required that "metropolitan areas, where conditions allow, should take the lead in mutual recognition of accumulative years required for obtaining local household registration, and accelerate the removal of household registration barriers between urban and rural areas." The mutual recognition in household registration in metropolitan areas shows the new direction for household registration reform. To promote the employment of migrant labor force, it is essential that the system and institutional barriers hindering the flow of labor and talents must be removed. China should continue with its household registration reform, transform migrants from rural areas to new urban residents, facilitate migrants' social integration, and ensure access to basic public services for all in urban areas.

Second, improve the social security system for migrants to satisfy their basic needs. Currently, the major problems with migrants' social insurance include some migrants failing to notice the importance of participating in social insurance, employers shirking their responsibilities, and difficulty of cross-region transfer and continuation of insurance accounts. Multiple parties involved, including employers, community organizations and supervisory authorities, should cooperate to promote participation in social insurance and motivate employers to pay for their employees' social insurance. Constant efforts should be made to expand migrants' participation in social insurance, improve the transfer and continuation of social insurance accounts, and enhance migrants' capacity to resist risks.

Third, while further promoting industrial restructuring, the government should monitor the employment situation of migrants and provide them with support. Where a number of enterprises go bankrupt in a short period of time, local governments should take proactive measures to pacify the people concerned and ensure their livelihoods. Most importantly, greater efforts are required to improve vocational training for migrants to enhance their ability to return to work. Possible measures include free vocational training and short-term training programs for adults. In response to the labor demand of specific industries, the government may arrange for vocational schools and employers to jointly provide training programs. The employment rate of vocational school graduates can serve as an assessment criterion in determining the financial support to vocational schools. Employment support for migrants is more than dealing with the legacy of shrinking industries. It also helps to satisfy the labor demand of emerging industries.

Fourth, provide migrants and their family members with access to urban public services to solve the worries of the migrant population. As migrants are staying longer in places of destination, there is an increasingly urgent need to satisfy the demands of their family members. The governments of migration destinations should meet the demands of migrant households in areas such as children's education, housing, health care, and social integration. Efforts should be accelerated to provide public services for women, children and the elderly in the migrant population, such as children's health care, preschool education, compulsory education, employment protection, health care and elderly care.

Bibliography

Duan, Chengrong, Liu Tao, and Lyu Lidan. "Migration Trends in China and the Implications." *Shandong Social Sciences*, no. 9 (2017): 63–69.

Duan, Chengrong, Yang Ge, and Zhang Fei. "Nine Trends in China's Migrants since the Start of Reform and Opening-up." *Population Research*, no. 6 (2008): 30–43.

Lyu, Lidan, Duan Chengrong, and Liu Tao. "An Analysis of the Change of Floating Population in China and the Implication." *South China Population*, no. 1 (2018).

Wang, Pei'an. "Migration Trends and Migration Studies in China's New Era." *Population Research*, no. 2 (2019): 3–5.

Yang, Ge. "Migration and Relative Poverty in Cities: Current Situation, Risk and Policy." *Review of Economy and Management*, no. 1 (2017).

Yang, Ge. "Respond Proactively to Changes in Migration and Mobility of Migrant Workers." *Guangming Daily*, June 13, 2019, page 15.

Yang, Juhua, Zhang Zhao, and Luo Yuying. "Migrant Generation in the Era of Migration: Changes in Characteristics of Young Migrants in China in the Past Three Decades." *China Youth Study*, no. 4 (2016).

Zelinsky, W. "The Hypothesis of the Mobility Transition." *Geographical Review*, no. 2 (1971).

CHAPTER 6

Changes in the Human Capital Structure of Migrant Workers: an Analysis of Existing College Graduates in China's Rural Migrants

Cai Yifei* and Gao Wenshu**

Existing college graduates in China's rural migrants refer to migrants with rural household registration who have entered the labor market after graduating from a junior college or a higher level of education. For a long period of time, this group of population has not drawn much attention. Following the expansion of higher education in China, especially the rapid development of junior colleges and higher vocational education, an increasing number of higher education graduates with rural household registration have entered the urban labor market, while their household registration remains in rural areas. The number of college-graduate-turned migrant workers has been rising fast, and stands at about twenty-eight million at present. Household registration policies concerning college graduates should pay attention to not only fresh graduates, but also the said population group. Measures should be adopted to encourage them to transfer their household registration from rural areas to urban areas where they are employed to raise the country's urbanization rate in terms of household registration.

1 An Overview of Existing College Graduates in China's Rural Migrants

Currently, about ten percent of China's rural migrants are college graduates, who are important members of the country's migrant workers. While the monitoring survey of migrant workers by the NBS and the CMDS by the National Health and Family Planning Commission of China are two nationally representative large-scale sample surveys, they are different, in that the NBS survey is conducted in migration origins and the CMDS in migration destinations.

* Cai Yifei is an associate professor at the Institute of Population and Labor Economics, CASS, and his research interests are regional economy and employment.

** Gao Wenshu is a professor at the School of Economics, University of Chinese Academy of Social Sciences(UCASS), and his research interests are human resources and employment.

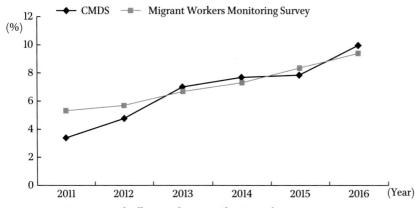

FIGURE 6.1   Proportion of college graduates in China's rural migrants

Survey respondents are selected from rural areas in the monitoring survey of the NBS and from urban areas in the CMDS. Calculation based on the CMDS data show that the proportion of college graduates, i.e., people with junior college and above education, in rural migrants was ten percent in 2016. The migrant workers monitoring survey by the NBS revealed a similar proportion of 9.4 percent. According to the NBS' monitoring survey of migrant workers in China, in 2016, the proportion of college graduates was 11.9 percent in migrant workers employed in places outside the towns of registered household residence, and 7.1 percent in those employed in towns of registered household residence.

The number of college graduates in China's rural migrants has been growing fast. As shown in Table 6.1, according to the CMDS by the National Health and Family Planning Commission, the proportion of college graduates in rural migrants increased from 3.4 percent in 2011 to ten percent in 2016, an increase of nearly seven percentage points. The monitoring survey of migrant workers by the NBS shows that the proportion of college graduates in migrant workers increased from 5.3 percent in 2011 to 9.4 percent in 2016, and the proportion of college graduates in migrant workers employed in places outside the towns of registered household residence rose from seven percent in 2011 to 11.9 percent in 2016 (see Table 6.2). Such changes are gradually altering the human capital composition of migrant workers in the traditional sense, and call for a new perception of migrant workers.

Against the backdrop of expanding higher education in China, the number of college graduates in the country hits a record high each year. Among these graduates are those of rural origin who are employed in cities but have not transferred their household registration to places where their schools are located or where they are employed. This has resulted in a rapid growth in college graduates with rural household registration in urban areas as they become

TABLE 6.1   Proportion of college graduates in migrants in China: based on the CMDS by the
National Health and Family Planning Commission

Year	In total migrant population (%)	In rural migrants (%)	In urban migrants (%)
2011	7.0	3.4	28.4
2012	9.1	4.8	34.1
2013	10.8	7.0	35.1
2014	13.6	7.7	41.5
2015	14.2	7.8	37.7
2016	15.8	10.0	42.9

Note: The National Health and Family Planning Commission of China has been conducting annually the CMDS in migration destinations across the country since 2009. The survey covers 180,000 migrant households and 500,000 migrants. Migrants in the survey include those from rural and urban areas, accounting for eighty-five percent and fifteen percent of the migrant population respectively. The respondents are aged sixteen and above.
SOURCE: CALCULATION BASED ON THE CMDS CONDUCTED BY THE DEPARTMENT OF MIGRANTS OF THE NATIONAL HEALTH AND FAMILY PLANNING COMMISSION

TABLE 6.2   Proportion of college graduates in migrants in China: based on the NBS'
monitoring survey of migrant workers

Year	In migrant workers (%)	In migrant workers employed outside towns of registered household residence (%)	In migrant workers employed in towns of registered household residence (%)
2011	5.3	7.0	3.4
2012	5.7	7.8	3.6
2013	6.7	8.2	5.1
2014	7.3	9.3	5.2
2015	8.3	10.7	6.0
2016	9.4	11.9	7.1

Note: The NBS of China has been conducting monitoring surveys of migrant workers in migration origins since 2008. The survey covers rural areas across the country and include samples of 8,906 villages and 237,000 rural workers from 1,527 surveyed counties and districts.
SOURCE: CALCULATION BASED ON *MIGRANT WORKERS MONITORING SURVEY REPORT* ISSUED BY THE NBS

migrant workers. To change this phenomenon, urgent efforts are required to speed up the household registration reform in China, especially to reform the policies about granting urban household registration to college graduates.

2 Composition of Existing College Graduates in China's Rural Migrants

There are no significant gender differences in the proportion of college graduates in China's rural migrants. The share of college graduates in female rural migrants is also around ten percent. According to the CMDS by the National Health and Family Planning Commission, the proportion of college graduates in China's female rural migrants increased rapidly from 3.2 percent in 2011 to 10.1 percent in 2016, slightly higher than that of male rural migrants, i.e., 9.9 percent (see Table 6.3). Thanks to the expansion of higher education, female students from rural areas have significantly better chances of attending junior colleges and universities, and the gender gap in rural migrants' human capital is also shrinking. Nonetheless, the proportion of college graduates in rural migrants, including female and male migrants, is still significantly lower than in urban-to-urban migrants, which is more than forty percent.

The proportion of college graduates is even higher in young rural migrants. In rural migrants below the age of thirty, the share of college graduates has exceeded twenty percent. According to the CMDS conducted by the National Health and Family Planning Commission in 2016, the share of college graduates was 24.2 percent in rural migrants aged twenty to twenty-four, and 20.3 percent

TABLE 6.3   Proportion of college graduates in migrants by gender

Year	Rural migrants		Urban migrants	
	Male (%)	Female (%)	Male (%)	Female (%)
2011	3.6	3.2	30.3	26.2
2012	5.0	4.5	36.0	32.1
2013	7.2	6.8	36.7	33.3
2014	7.9	7.5	42.9	40.0
2015	7.9	7.7	39.4	36.0
2016	9.9	10.1	44.1	41.6

SOURCE: CALCULATION BASED ON THE CMDS CONDUCTED BY THE DEPARTMENT OF MIGRANTS OF THE NATIONAL HEALTH AND FAMILY PLANNING COMMISSION

TABLE 6.4   Proportion of college graduates in China's migrants in 2016 by age group

Age (years)	Rural migrants (%)	Urban migrants (%)
15–19	6.2	12.8
20–24	24.2	59.1
25–29	20.3	64.1
30–34	12.8	64.8
35–39	5.7	48.0
40–44	1.9	27.8
45–49	0.8	18.5
50–54	0.5	14.3
55–59	0.3	12.1
60+	0.4	13.8

SOURCE: CALCULATION BASED ON THE CMDS CONDUCTED BY THE DEPARTMENT OF MIGRANTS OF THE NATIONAL HEALTH AND FAMILY PLANNING COMMISSION

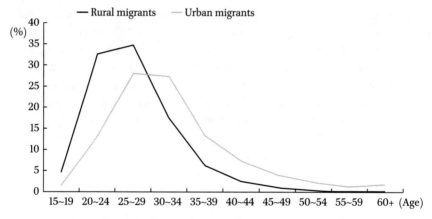

FIGURE 6.2   Composition of college graduates in China's migrants in 2016 by age

in those aged twenty-five to twenty-nine (see Table 6.4). On average, there is a college graduate out of four to five young migrant workers. The share of college graduates in older migrant workers aged above thirty-five, however, is very low, and it is less than one percent in those aged above forty-five.

College-graduate-turned migrant workers are typical young migrant workers. An analysis of the surveys shows that seventy-two percent of college graduates in China's rural migrants are under the age of thirty, and some ninety percent are under the age of thirty-five. In terms of year of birth, the

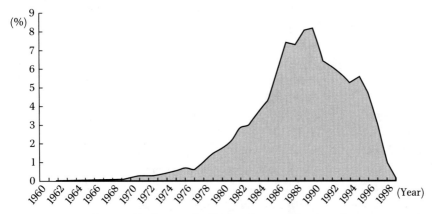

FIGURE 6.3 Distribution of birth years of college graduates in China's rural migrants in 2016

new generation of migrant workers born in 1980 is the main source of college graduates in rural migrants. Among the college graduates in China's rural migrants, ninety-three percent were born after 1980, and forty-six percent were born after 1990. This suggests great differences between generations of rural migrants in human capital. College-graduate-turned migrant workers reflect the characteristics of young migrant workers in China. College graduates in rural migrants are typical young migrant workers. The issue of granting urban household registration to these people is in essence about the treatment of high-quality young migrant workers.

College graduates in China's rural migrants are largely graduates of junior colleges, but the proportion of people with a bachelor's or higher degree is on the rise. According to the CMDS conducted by the National Health and Family Planning Commission, junior college graduates account for some seventy percent of the college graduates in rural migrants, and people with a bachelor's degree account for about thirty percent. The proportion of people with a bachelor's or higher degree is higher in urban migrants, about fifty percent. The proportion of rural migrants with a bachelor's degree or higher has shown an upward trend, growing from twenty-two percent in 2011 to more than thirty percent in 2016 (see Table 6.5). The increase shows that more college graduates in China's rural migrants have received a higher level of tertiary education.

The rising proportion of rural migrants who have received higher education is causing changes in the human capital structure of migrant workers in the traditional sense. Traditionally, migrant workers are considered low skilled and poorly educated. Due to the rapid expansion of higher education and the slow reform of household registration policies targeting college graduates, however, the past few years have witnessed a fast-changing composition of China's

TABLE 6.5   Composition of college graduates in China's migrants by educational attainment

Year	2011 (%)	2012 (%)	2013 (%)	2014 (%)	2015 (%)	2016 (%)
	College graduates in rural migrants					
Junior college	77.8	73.0	68.5	73.7	71.9	68.7
Bachelor's degree	21.7	26.3	29.9	25.5	27.1	30.1
Master's degree	0.5	0.7	1.7	0.8	1.0	1.2
	College graduates in urban migrants					
Junior college	59.0	54.8	54.6	53.1	51.9	49.4
Bachelor's degree	37.6	41.2	41.7	42.2	43.1	44.8
Master's degree	3.4	4.0	3.8	4.8	5.0	5.8

SOURCE: CALCULATED BASED ON THE CMDS CONDUCTED BY THE DEPARTMENT OF
MIGRANTS OF THE NATIONAL HEALTH AND FAMILY PLANNING COMMISSION

migrant workers. As shown in Table 6.6, the proportion of migrant workers with an educational attainment at high school level or lower has been falling, while that of migrant workers with junior college and above education is gradually increasing. According to the CMDS conducted by the National Health and Family Planning Commission, the proportion of rural migrants with junior high school and primary school education dropped from 58.7 percent and 17.5 percent in 2011 to 50.2 percent and 15.5 percent in 2016, while that of rural migrants with junior college education and a bachelor's degree increased from 2.6 percent and 0.7 percent to 6.9 percent and 3.0 percent. This period also saw a small number of rural migrants with a master's degree.

The proportion of college graduates in migrants varies among provinces. It is comparatively higher in the developed central and eastern regions of China. The CMDS conducted by the National Health and Family Planning Commission shows that Beijing has the highest proportion, 11.2 percent, of college graduates in rural migrants, but the figure is still lower than the proportion of sixty percent in urban migrants. The proportion of college graduates in rural migrants is close to ten percent in Shandong, Hunan and Shaanxi, and about nine percent in Jiangsu, Henan, Chongqing and Shanghai. It is lower in China's northeast and western regions. For example, the proportion is 3.6 percent in Heilongjiang, and about four percent in Qinghai, Tibet, Guizhou and Yunnan. It is also important to note that in economically developed Zhejiang and Guangdong, where there is a large influx of migrant workers, the proportion of college graduates in rural migrants is respectively 4.5 percent and 6.7 percent, which are not high. This may be attributable to the highly developed

TABLE 6.6   Composition of China's migrants by educational attainment

Educational attainment	2011 (%)	2012 (%)	2013 (%)	2014 (%)	2015 (%)	2016 (%)
			Rural migrants			
Illiterate	2.3	2.8	2.0	2.1	2.7	2.4
Primary school	17.5	16.7	14.5	15.0	15.8	15.5
Junior secondary school	58.7	55.8	55.2	54.9	52.5	50.2
Senior secondary school / secondary vocational school	18.1	20.0	21.3	20.3	21.3	21.9
Junior college	2.6	3.5	4.8	5.7	5.6	6.9
Bachelor's degree	0.7	1.3	2.1	2.0	2.1	3.0
Master's degree	0.0	0.0	0.1	0.1	0.1	0.1
			Urban migrants			
Illiterate	0.7	0.8	0.6	0.6	1.0	0.7
Primary school	5.2	4.5	4.1	4.1	5.9	4.8
Junior secondary school	32.4	28.4	28.3	25.1	26.0	23.6
Senior secondary school / secondary vocational school	33.3	32.3	32.0	28.7	29.4	28.0
Junior college	16.7	18.7	19.1	22.0	19.6	21.2
Bachelor's degree	10.7	14.1	14.6	17.5	16.3	19.2
Master's degree	1.0	1.4	1.3	2.0	1.9	2.5

SOURCE: CALCULATION BASED ON THE CMDS CONDUCTED BY THE DEPARTMENT OF MIGRANTS OF THE NATIONAL HEALTH AND FAMILY PLANNING COMMISSION

TABLE 6.7   Proportion of college graduates in migrants by place

Code	Place	Rural migrants (%)	Urban migrants (%)	Total migrant population (%)
11	Beijing	11.2	59.6	28.8
12	Tianjin	5.4	44.7	11.0
13	Hebei	7.2	38.9	11.8
14	Shanxi	5.8	38.8	11.0
15	Inner Mongolia	8.3	35.3	12.7
21	Liaoning	6.5	30.3	13.7
22	Jilin	6.0	23.6	9.7
23	Heilongjiang	3.6	17.7	6.9

TABLE 6.7   Proportion of college graduates in migrants by place (*cont.*)

Code	Place	Rural migrants (%)	Urban migrants (%)	Total migrant population (%)
31	Shanghai	8.8	52.2	20.1
32	Jiangsu	9.7	42.0	14.3
33	Zhejiang	4.5	36.2	7.8
34	Anhui	7.5	35.8	12.5
35	Fujian	7.4	35.8	10.4
36	Jiangxi	6.7	31.9	10.9
37	Shandong	11.0	40.1	14.3
41	Henan	9.1	38.9	11.7
42	Hubei	7.6	33.0	10.6
43	Hunan	10.0	30.3	12.5
44	Guangdong	6.7	38.6	12.7
45	Guangxi	7.9	38.5	12.9
46	Hainan	5.7	32.5	11.8
50	Chongqing	9.0	35.2	16.9
51	Sichuan	7.6	34.1	13.2
52	Guizhou	4.1	30.1	9.1
53	Yunnan	4.4	26.8	6.6
54	Tibet	4.0	14.4	5.0
61	Shaanxi	9.9	41.0	13.0
62	Gansu	6.4	36.3	10.6
63	Qinghai	3.9	28.1	6.7
64	Ningxia	4.5	32.8	7.9
65	Xinjiang	5.6	32.7	10.5
66	Xinjiang Production and Construction Corps	4.2	26.1	7.1

SOURCE: CALCULATION BASED ON THE CMDS CONDUCTED BY THE DEPARTMENT OF MIGRANTS OF THE NATIONAL HEALTH AND FAMILY PLANNING COMMISSION

traditional manufacturing industries in these provinces. Thanks to the great job creation potential of these industries, a huge number of low-skilled rural migrants with a low level of educational attainment are attracted to these provinces to find a job.

3   Estimate of the Number of Existing College Graduates in China's Rural Migrants

Currently, there are about twenty-eight million college graduates in China's rural migrants. The estimation is based on the surveys conducted by the NBS and the National Health and Family Planning Commission. According to the number of migrant workers employed in and outside the towns of registered household residence published in the NBS' *Migrant Workers Monitoring Survey Report*, and the proportion of college graduates in these migrant workers respectively, at the end of 2016, the number of college graduates was about 20.15 million in migrant workers employed outside the towns of registered household residence, about eight million in migrant workers employed in the towns of registered household residence, and about 28.13 million in all migrant workers (see Table 6.8). According to the proportion of college graduates in migrants based on the CMDS of the National Health and Family Planning Commission and the total number of migrant workers in China, at the end of 2016, there were about 28.11 million college graduates in China's rural migrants (see Table 6.9). The estimates based on the surveys conducted by the NBS and the National Health and Family Planning Commission do not show a major difference. Both reveal that currently, there are about twenty-eight million college graduates among China's rural migrants. The number of college graduates in China's rural migrants has been growing rapidly in the past few years. The estimates based on the NBS' monitoring survey show that the number increased from fourteen million in 2011 to more than twenty million in 2014, and increased by 1.4 times in 2016 from the level in 2011. If the rising trend continues, there will be more than thirty million college graduates in China's rural migrants in 2017.

If all household registration restrictions are lifted for existing college graduates in China's rural migrants and all these people are granted urban household registration through reform of relevant policies and policy incentives, the urbanization rate of registered population in China will increase by about two percentage points. According to the Ministry of Public Security of China, the urbanization rate of China's registered population was 41.2 percent in 2016. If the twenty-eight million college graduates in rural migrants are granted urban household registration, the urbanization rate will climb to about 43.5 percent.

The number of both female and male college graduates in China's rural migrants stands at about fourteen million. Nearly twenty million of these people are under the age of thirty. The number of college graduates in rural migrants of different age groups is estimated based on the CMDS of the National

TABLE 6.8   Estimate of the number of college graduates in China's migrants based on the
              monitoring survey of migrant workers by the NBS

Year	Number of migrant workers employed outside towns of registered household residence	Number of migrant workers employed in towns of reg- istered household residence	Number of college graduates in migrant workers employed outside towns of registered household residence	Number of college graduates in migrant workers employed in towns of registered household residence	Number of college graduates in rural migrants
2011	158.63	94.15	11.10	3.20	14.31
2012	163.36	99.25	12.74	3.57	16.32
2013	166.10	102.84	13.62	5.24	18.87
2014	168.21	105.74	15.64	5.50	21.14
2015	168.84	108.63	18.07	6.52	24.58
2016	169.34	112.37	20.15	7.98	28.13

Unit: Million
SOURCE: CALCULATION BASED ON THE *MIGRANT WORKERS MONITORING SURVEY REPORT*
ISSUED BY THE NBS

TABLE 6.9   Estimate of college graduates in China's rural migrants based on the CMDS by the
              National Health and Family Planning Commission

Year	Proportion of college graduates in rural migrants (%)	Number of migrant workers in China	Number of college graduates in China's migrant workers
2011	3.4	252.78	8.54
2012	4.8	262.61	12.50
2013	7.0	268.94	18.80
2014	7.7	273.95	21.07
2015	7.8	277.47	21.64
2016	10.0	281.71	28.11

Unit: Million
SOURCE: CALCULATION BASED ON THE CMDS CONDUCTED BY THE DEPARTMENT OF
MIGRANTS OF THE NATIONAL HEALTH AND FAMILY PLANNING COMMISSION

TABLE 6.10   Estimate of the number of college graduates in China's rural migrants in 2016 by
age groups

Age (years)	Proportion (%)	Total number	Male	Female
15–19	4.2	1.19	0.60	0.59
20–24	27.5	7.72	4.25	3.48
25–29	37.4	10.52	5.60	4.92
30–34	19.9	5.60	2.53	3.07
35–39	7.1	2.00	0.73	1.27
40–44	2.5	0.69	0.20	0.49
45–49	0.9	0.25	0.07	0.18
50–54	0.3	0.08	0.01	0.07
55–59	0.1	0.02	0.01	0.01
60+	0.1	0.03	0.01	0.02
Sum	100.0	28.10	14.00	14.10

Unit: Million
SOURCE: CALCULATION BASED ON THE CMDS CONDUCTED BY THE DEPARTMENT OF
MIGRANTS OF THE NATIONAL HEALTH AND FAMILY PLANNING COMMISSION

Health and Family Planning Commission, which shows that young college graduates account for a large proportion of the total. As shown in Table 6.10, there are nearly twenty million college graduates in rural migrants under the age of thirty. That includes 7.72 million aged between twenty and twenty-four, and more than ten million aged between twenty-five and twenty-nine. On the other hand, there are only more than one million people aged over forty among the college graduates in China's rural migrants.

College graduates in China's rural migrants largely concentrate in the country's economically developed eastern region. Estimates based on the CMDS of the National Health and Family Planning Commission and the NBS' monitoring survey of migrant workers show that among the twenty-eight million college graduates in China's rural migrants, nearly sixteen million are in the economically developed eastern region, 5.5 million are in the central region, another 5.5 million are in the western region, and less than one million are in the northeast (see Figure 6.4). In terms of the distribution of these people, Guangdong has the largest number of college graduates in rural migrants, which is nearly five million. The number is about two million in both Jiangsu and Zhejiang, about 1.6 million in Shanghai, more than 1.2 million in Beijing, Shandong and Sichuan, and around or below 200,000 in Tibet, Qinghai, Ningxia, and Hainan.

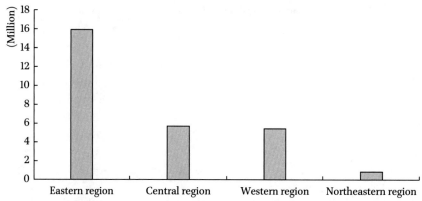

FIGURE 6.4 Estimate of the number of college graduates in China's rural migrants in
different regions in 2016

TABLE 6.11 Estimate of the number of college graduates in migrants in different places of
China in 2016

Code	Place	Proportion in migrants (%)	Number of college graduates in rural migrants (million)
11	Beijing	4.6	1.287
12	Tianjin	2.2	0.627
13	Hebei	2.4	0.671
14	Shanxi	2.0	0.551
15	Inner Mongolia	2.2	0.624
21	Liaoning	2.8	0.775
22	Jilin	1.3	0.378
23	Heilongjiang	1.5	0.409
31	Shanghai	5.6	1.573
32	Jiangsu	7.4	2.076
33	Zhejiang	7.3	2.040
34	Anhui	2.9	0.810
35	Fujian	4.2	1.168
36	Jiangxi	1.5	0.409
37	Shandong	4.7	1.327
41	Henan	3.0	0.848
42	Hubei	3.9	1.087
43	Hunan	3.0	0.852

TABLE 6.11   Estimate of the number of college graduates in migrants (*cont.*)

Code	Place	Proportion in migrants (%)	Number of college graduates in rural migrants (million)
44	Guangdong	17.6	4.941
45	Guangxi	2.2	0.626
46	Hainan	0.8	0.217
50	Chongqing	1.9	0.532
51	Sichuan	4.9	1.385
52	Guizhou	1.7	0.482
53	Yunnan	2.3	0.642
54	Tibet	0.2	0.052
61	Shaanxi	2.4	0.674
62	Gansu	1.0	0.292
63	Qinghai	0.4	0.112
64	Ningxia	0.5	0.141
65	Xinjiang	1.8	0.492

SOURCE: CALCULATION BASED ON THE CMDS CONDUCTED BY THE DEPARTMENT OF MIGRANTS OF THE NATIONAL HEALTH AND FAMILY PLANNING COMMISSION AND THE ONE-PERCENT NATIONAL POPULATION SURVEY BY THE NBS IN 2015

4   Policy Responses to Existing College Graduates in China's Rural Migrants

The rapid expansion of higher education and outdated household registration policies targeting college graduates in China have jointly led to the appearance of college-graduate-turned migrant workers. This is an important issue that calls for urgent attention and solution in China's current household registration reform. According to the nationally representative migrant monitoring survey conducted by the NBS and the CMDS by the National Health and Family Planning Commission, currently, college graduates account for about ten percent of China's rural migrants, and the number of college-graduate-turned migrant workers has reached twenty-eight million. The number is still growing rapidly. College graduates with rural household registration have become an important part of migrant workers in China. This calls for a change in the traditional perception of migrant workers as low skilled and poorly educated. It is also necessary to introduce new ways to reform the household registration system, and work faster to grant urban household registration to college graduates of rural household registration.

A new perception should be created to treat college graduates with rural household registration as valuable human resources. All household registration restrictions should be lifted to ensure that the existing college graduates with rural household registration can directly obtain urban household registration. Except in a few special big cities such as Beijing and Shanghai, all cities should abolish the household registration threshold for college graduates, and people with at least an associate degree should be entitled to household registration in the cities they live. A few megacities with point-based household registration policies should give more weight and points to the applicants' education background to help high-quality workers find a job and obtain local household registration. Policies on college graduates' household registration shall apply to both new and old graduates. With all household registration restrictions lifted for existing college graduates of rural household registration, and through reform of relevant policies and policy incentives, the twenty-eight million college graduates of rural household registration will obtain urban household registration. In that case, China's urbanization rate of registered population will increase by two percentage points to about 43.5 percent, and will reach the target of forty-five percent by 2020.

In design of strategies, a clear picture of the deep-lying issues in China's household registration reform is required. Measures should be phased in to grant urban household registration to relevant college graduates and to advance the urbanization of registered population. For higher urbanization rate of registered population in China, attention should be paid to both practical institutional barriers and objective economic laws so as to address the fundamental causes of the difficulty in obtaining household registration in certain places and the lack of interest in household registration in some other places.[1] Medium-sized cities in China, mainly provincial capitals, play a crucial role in the country's efforts to significantly raise its urbanization rate of registered population. They need to further and decisively relax their household registration restrictions to allow college graduates to make household registration decisions according to their wishes without considering other conditions. In general, household registration reform is an increase in net welfare, but the

---

1   Cheng Jie, "The Source of City Vitality: The Systematic Effects of Migrants on City's Economic Development," *Urban and Environmental Studies*, 4(2018), 56–71.

key problem is the inequality and inequivalence in the distribution of costs and benefits. The key to household registration reform is thus a good cost-sharing mechanism. The central government needs to bear a larger share and increase the incentives for local governments.[2]

----

2   Qu Xiaobo, and Cheng Jie, "Degree of Association between Regional Disparity, Urbanization and the Cost of Household Registration Reform," *Reform*, 3(2013), 37–44.

CHAPTER 7

Changes in China Arising from the New Technological Revolution and the Trends as Shown in the Competition between Humans and Robots

*Qu Xiaobo**

The Fourth Industrial Revolution, or Industry 4.0, represented by the use of robots and AI, has started. The spread and extensive use of new technologies have become an unstoppable trend in a new round of automation and upgrade. It is profoundly affecting and changing the employment structure, job tasks and returns to skill in China's labor market. This study examines and analyzes the impact of the new technological revolution and automation on China's labor market and the changes and trends in the labor market by examining the effect of the new technological revolution on economic growth. From a historical perspective of economic development and technological progress, robots and AI represent a new stage of economic growth driven by automation, which may cause increasing marginal returns to scale and affect the micro behavior of enterprises. AI technologies can alleviate China's labor shortage, improve its productivity, and boost its economic growth.

1   New Technological Revolution, Automation and Economic Growth

Economists have been following the economic and social impact of technological revolution. But the new technological revolution represented by robots and AI have broken the laws of increasing marginal cost or diminishing returns to investment for capital in economic development. That means, besides preparation for a zero marginal cost society proposed by Jeremy Rifkin, it is essential to better understand the possibility of an increasing marginal returns to scale.[1] It is about the significance of the new technological revolution. How does AI affect economic growth? As suggested by the model of Zeira,

---

* Qu Xiaobo is an associate professor at the Institute of Population and Labor Economics, CASS, and his research interests are labor economics and employment.
[1]   Cai Fang, "A Myth of Two Economics: Embracing the New Technological Revolution?" *Studies in Labor Economics*, 2 (2019), 3–20.

another part of technological progress is the automation of production.[2] From a historical perspective, mankind's economic growth in the past 150 years has been driven by automation. From the adoption of steam engines in the First Industrial Revolution, to mass production enabled by electricity in the Second Industrial Revolution, to the computer revolution resulting from the use of semiconductors, computers and the Internet in the Third Industrial Revolution, automation of production has remained a major characteristic of economic growth.[3] AI is the next stage of automation, which will enable automatic cruise, computer-controlled automobile engines and MRI machines, and AI in radiology. It is generally agreed that the Fourth Industrial Revolution represented by the use of robots and AI has started. From such an analytical perspective, AI can be considered a new form of automation in the new technological revolution, which allows automation of tasks that used to be impossible. Due to the close connection between automation and Baumol's cost disease,[4] while the agricultural and manufacturing sectors are growing rapidly thanks to automation, their shares in GDP are falling because of the price reduction and lower elasticity of substitution of their products manufactured through automation.

The global demand for AI technologies will continue to grow, and AI is expected to contribute 15.7 trillion US dollars to the global economy by 2030. McKinsey claims in a report that, deep learning, the most advanced form of machine learning, will create trillions of US dollars of potential economic value, and that China and North America will enjoy great economic gains from AI: by 2030, AI will contribute to twenty-six percent of China's GDP growth and 14.5 percent of the economic growth in North America.[5] Such development prospect is primarily based on national development strategies, the backbone of which consists of AI, big data and the Internet.

Nonetheless, the development of AI and its macroeconomic effect depend on a large number of potential micro behaviors of enterprises. First, AI affects innovation and growth through potential competitiveness in the goods market. While AI makes imitation of existing products and technologies easier, it may also cause potential innovators to invent new product lines to avoid

2   Joseph Zeira, "Workers, Machines, and Economic Growth," *Quarterly Journal of Economics* 113, 4 (1998), 1091–1117.
3   Zeira (1998) and Acemoglu & Restrepo (2016) both include automation in the analytical framework of production functions.
4   William J. Baumol, "Macroeconomics of Unbalanced Growth: The Anatomy of Urban Crisis," *American Economic Review* 57, (1967), 415–426.
5   Milena Kabza, "Artificial Intelligence Supports Economic Growth," March 26, 2019, https://financialobserver.eu/poland/artificial-intelligence-supports-economic-growth/.

competition and imitation of existing lines in a sector.[6] That being the case, the overall growth effect will depend on the relative contribution of primary innovation, aiming at creating new products, and secondary innovation in a sector to the overall growth. AI and digital revolution also affect innovation and growth by influencing the degree of competition in the goods market relevant to the development of networks and platforms. The primary goal of platform suppliers is to strengthen their monopoly by maximizing the size of suppliers and demanders in the market. Second, the revolution of information technology has created an important knowledge diffusion effect.[7] Knowledge diffusion leads to reallocation across sectors, in which knowledge diffuses from sectors that do not rely heavily on technology externalities, such as the textile industry, to those with a heavy dependence on technology externalities. This also applies to AI. Knowledge diffusion among firms and sectors makes it easier for firms to learn from each other and make profit. Meanwhile, AI technologies improve the spread of knowledge among firms and sectors. Therefore, in addition to its immediate effect on enterprises' innovation and capacity, AI also enhances the reallocation effect among sectors.

Over the past four decades since the start of reform and opening-up, China has enjoyed a comparative advantage of demographic dividend in its economic development. Seizing the opportunity of globalization to further open up to the outside world, China has seen significant economic growth with an expanding labor force. However, China is losing the said growth driver due to population ageing amid a rapid demographic transition. In view of the demographic trends in China, if its productivity remains at the current level, China will not have adequate labor to maintain economic growth. The only way to maintain its economic growth is to raise productivity significantly. New AI technologies can narrow the gap between productivity improvement and labor shortage. It mitigates labor shortage by assisting and replacing workers. An AI system can help people perform existing tasks more efficiently, thereby improving productivity. AI makes manufacturing, supply chains, logistics and other production and service processes of the manufacturing sector more efficient, and creates greater profits by predicting failures, identifying bottlenecks and automated processes and decision-making. According to McKinsey Global Institute,[8] AI-led automation will raise the productivity in China's agriculture,

---

6 Nicholas Bloom, Luis Garicano, Raffaella Sadun, and John Van Reenen, "The Distinct Effects of Information Technology and Communication Technology on Firm Organization," *Management Science* 60, 12 (2014), 2859–2885.

7 Salome Baslandze, "The Role of the IT Revolution in Knowledge Diffusion, Innovation and Reallocation," *EIEF Manuscript*.

8 McKinsey Global Institute, *Artificial Intelligence: Implications for China* (March 2017).

manufacturing, accommodation and food services and add 0.8 to 1.4 percentage points to its economic growth annually. The extensive adoption of AI technologies will improve the country's productivity and boost its economic growth.

2 Robots and AI, and Job Tasks and Skills

Amid the new technological revolution of automation, the human workforce tend to be replaced by robots and AI in routine job tasks and occupations. Workers performing codifiable repetitive tasks are most vulnerable. According to a survey by the World Economic Forum in 2018,[9] currently, the task hours performed by machines account for twenty-nine percent of the total, which is expected to rise to forty-two percent by 2022, while the share of task hours performed by humans will drop from seventy-one percent to fifty-eight percent. Upon graduating from a four-year Bachelor of Science or Engineering program, people will find that nearly half of the knowledge they learnt in their freshman year has become obsolete. That means, in addition to the disappearance of old occupations and appearance of new ones, traditional occupations are also evolving into new ones requiring multiple skills. In Guangdong, Jiangsu and Zhejiang, traditional industries are undergoing transformation and upgrading by adopting AI and replacing humans with machines, resulting in increasingly digitalized and smart manufacturing, distribution and sales. Some enterprises in these provinces have reduced their workforce by thirty to forty percent in the past three years.[10]

In retrospect we see not only ubiquitous automation, but also a continuous generation of new tasks and new jobs for the labor force. First, the replacement of humans by machines generates a greater labor demand and creates new jobs. Second, the much-discussed productivity effect of automation reduces the production cost of job tasks, and increases the demand for labor for job tasks that are not automated.[11] Bessen (2016) gave a good example in this regard with the impact of ATMs on the employment of bank tellers.[12] In his opinion, ATMs reduced the operating costs of banks and encouraged the establishment of more bank branches, which increased the demand

9   World Economic Forum, *The Future of Jobs Report 2018*.
10   China Development Research Foundation, *Artificial Intelligence and the Future of Work in China (White Paper)*.
11   David, H. Autor, "Why are There Still So Many Jobs? The History and Future of Workplace Automation," *Journal of Economic Perspectives* 29, 3 (2015), 3–30.
12   James Bessen, *Learning by Doing: The Real Connection between Innovation, Wages, and Wealth.* (New Haven: Yale University Press, 2016).

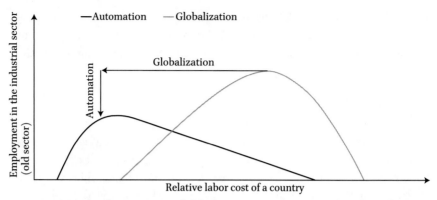

FIGURE 7.1   Impact of automation and globalization on employment in the industrial sector

for tellers performing tasks that could not be automated and performed by ATMs. Productivity improvement also raises real income, thus resulting in a greater consumption demand for, inter alia, goods and services that are not automated. The negative displacement effect of automation is thus offset by a greater demand from other industries.

Judging from theoretical models, when labor costs exceed a certain level, enterprises have to resort to automation of production – adoption of robots, or transfer jobs to countries with lower labor costs (see Figure 7.1). Accordingly, while China is shifting from labor-intensive, low-cost manufacturing to high-skilled, technology-intensive production, it needs to compete with not only capital-intensive rivals from developing countries with higher labor costs, but also technology-intensive manufacturers from Asian and East European countries with moderate labor costs. Such cost reduction is achieved through automation within enterprises or indirectly through market competition. This is an inevitable challenge China has to confront as its demographic dividend is waning and its population is ageing. AI presents an important opportunity for China to stand up to this challenge and boost its productivity growth. In addition to improving productivity, the development of AI will also create new products and services, and will lead to new jobs and tasks. AI will cause similar changes the way information technology has enabled the Internet economy and created new occupations.

The development of new technologies, mainly robotics and AI, has created many new jobs, which is changing the labor market. Compared with previous technological progress, AI will replace more jobs, including brain workers, because it also enables the automation of brainwork. On the one hand, AI improves work efficiency in a way different from previous automation technologies and computers. With machine learning and common learning strategies,

AI can read a massive amount of big data, find patterns, connections and new insights from the data, and automatically adjust to data updates without the need for reprogramming. AI is thus capable of induction, reasoning and decision-making as humans are.[13] On the other hand, technological progress in AI has reduced costs and prices, thereby creating new demand for labor and jobs. Take the education industry as an example. With the existing technologies, providing private educational services and personalized tutoring services to a small group of students would incur high educational costs. The adoption of AI may make such educational services accessible to more people,[14] and create more educational tasks, such as supervision, monitoring, design, and implementation of private education programs. Similar demand for labor and jobs is also growing rapidly in healthcare and elderly care industries.

The new technological revolution represented by robots and AI is bringing new job tasks and changing existing tasks, leading to demand for new skills. It is redefining the job skills required. Skills are the key to matching supply and demand in the labor market. They reflect the demand and supply in the labor market better than occupations and degrees, because the expertise and skills required for a certain occupation are changing increasingly fast, and degrees tend to become obsolete upon acquisition. The current technological revolution caters to a dynamic market that values skills over degrees. A LinkedIn report in 2018 based on data of 630 million people from around the world with more than 35,000 skills reveals skills that are more common in a certain area than in others. The top ten fastest growing jobs over the past four years are all middle- and high-level management jobs in areas such as customer service, marketing, finance, products, operation and so on.[15] The fastest growing skills fall into four categories. First, functional skills such as marketing, customer service and so on, which reflect one's communication ability. Second, leadership and other soft skills, analytical and communication skills required for non-routine analytical job tasks. Third, digital skills such as proficiency in social media and so on, which reflect one's cognitive and communication

---

13   AI technologies as mentioned generally comprise four parts, namely cognition (processing of language and computer videos and audios), prediction (such as prediction of behavior and results in advertising targeted at a certain group of customers), decision-making (route planning, R&D of new drugs, dynamic pricing) and integrated solution (autonomous driving and robotic surgery). They will have a profound impact on job tasks and jobs.

14   The market size of online education in China was 250 billion yuan in 2018.

15   Some once-niche jobs have become familiar to the public. An example is new media directors of operations many of whom introduced themselves as website editors five years ago.

ability. Fourth, English and other value-added skills, which reflect one's cognitive ability. The growing demand for these skills shows that more and more skills are closely linked to the new technological revolution. Therefore, policy-making and employment promotion authorities need to adopt skills as an analytical variable and provide effective analytical tools for the adjustment to employment decisions and labor market institutions, so as to help workers prepare for the future while improving their resilience.

The new technological revolution has changed the demand for three types of skills.[16] First, the demand for cognitive skills, communication skills and social behavior skills for nonrepetitive jobs has been rising in both developed and emerging economies. Second, the demand for skills required for repetitive jobs is declining. Third, the demand for combination of skills is also increasing. Workers are required to have multiple skills to be more adaptable, so that they can change their jobs and adapt to new ones. When one talks about such changes, it is not only about the replacement of old jobs with new ones, but also about the changing combination of existing job skills. What is required is no longer a separate skill, but a combination of cognitive skills, communication skills, social behavior skills, language skills, computer skills and other manual skills. Non-repetitive tasks, such as teamworking, relationship management, personnel management, and caregiving, require workers with analytical skills, interpersonal skills or manual skills with considerable dexterity. Therefore, robots can assist these workers with their tasks and help them to perform their tasks more efficiently. Autor and Dorn (2013) pointed out in their research that tasks such as education, designing, art, research, team management, caregiving, cleaning and so on cannot be automated.[17] It is difficult for robots to copy such skills to compete with humans. Even in a specific industry, the impact of technology on the skills required for a job is also changing, though the change is not always as people have expected. For example, the adoption of complex computer software for client management and firm operations in Chile between 2007 and 2013 caused a decline in firm's demand for workers performing abstract tasks and an increase in their demand for workers performing repetitive manual tasks.[18] It thus led to reassignment of skilled workers to administrative and unskilled production work.

---

16   Daron Acemoglu, and David H. Autor, "Skills, Tasks, and Technologies: Implications for Employment and Earnings," in Orley C. Ashenfelter, and David Card, ed. *Handbook of Labor Economics* 4B, (Elsevier, 2011), 1043–1171.

17   David H. Autor, and David Dorn, "The Growth of Low-Skill Service Jobs and the Polarization of the US Labor Market," *American Economic Review* 103, 5 (2013), 1553–1597.

18   Rita K. Almeida, Ana M. Fernandes, and Mariana Viollaz, "Does the Adoption of Complex Software Impact Employment Composition and the Skill Content of Occupations?

An understanding of AI's impact on future job tasks and occupations will keep policymakers informed about what jobs are created by new technologies, what jobs are being replaced, and the skills required in view of such employment changes, so that they can find future career paths for workers facing a declining labor demand. A distinctive characteristic of the new technological revolution is that as the scale of technology adoption continues to expand and the costs of new technologies decrease, new sectors and new job tasks are emerging, which will compensate to some extent for the reduction of routine jobs in traditional fields, although new technologies will change the way these jobs evolve. Insight into the changing demand for skills will help education and training services to adapt their programme and positioning to emerging skill trends.

3   Effects of the New Technological Revolution on Employment and Wages in China's Labor Market

Economists have summarized the theoretical models about the effects of automation and AI on labor demand, wages and employment,[19] while stressing the constraints and imperfections that slow down the economic adjustment and the adjustment of the labor market to automation. The displacement of labor by machine- and AI-enabled automation in some job tasks reduces the demand for labor and wages. But this displacement effect is counteracted by a productivity effect of automation as automation reduces costs and thus increases the demand for labor in non-automated job tasks. The productivity effect is complemented by additional capital accumulation and the deepening of automation, both of which further raise the demand for labor. These countervailing effects, however, are uncertain. The output per worker generated by automation exceeds that of the reduction in the share of labor in national income. The more powerful countervailing effect is new labor-intensive job tasks created by automation.

It is difficult to make an accurate forecast of the extent to which new technologies will displace workers and its impact on future employment, because it remains a challenge for economists to quantify the impact of technological progress on job displacement. Some researches show that AI and related

Evidence from Chilean Firms," in *Policy Research Working Paper 8110* (Washington, DC: World Bank, 2017); World Economic Forum, *The Future of Jobs Report 2018*.

19   Daron Acemoglu, and Pascual Restrepo, "Artificial Intelligence, Automation and Work", *NBER Working Paper No. 24196*.

technologies can replace low-skilled workers performing routine tasks, but they will also create many new jobs as productivity is improved, technologies are adopted and costs are reduced. From 1999 to 2016, for example, the technological revolution led to more than twenty-three million new jobs in Europe while it replaced workers performing routine tasks. Evidence from Europe shows that technology may replace some workers, but in general it increases the demand for labor.[20] Technological advancement not only creates jobs directly in the technology sector, but also enables people to increase their use of smartphones, tablets and other portable electronic devices to perform their job tasks. Technology facilitates job creation through online work and participation in the gig economy. Thanks to China's huge population and complete industrial structure, it has access to a massive amount of data and enjoys enormous market potential, making it one of the world's major hubs of AI development.

It is difficult to ascertain the jobs lost due to the new technological revolution, especially in China where there is an enormous labor force and considerable regional disparities in development. As the adoption of AI systems is closely connected with labor costs, it is hard to estimate how fast AI can enable a thorough transformation of traditional industries. According to McKinsey Global Institute, China has more workers than other countries performing automatable job tasks, with an automation potential of fifty-one percent, equivalent to 394 million full time employees.[21] PwC (2018) is more optimistic, and claims that the net impact of AI on jobs in China will raise productivity and real income and create a lot of new jobs. According to PwC, the additional jobs created by new technologies in China in the following two decades may account for twelve percent of the existing number of jobs in China, equivalent to around ninety million new jobs. These new jobs will not be distributed evenly across all sectors, and their net impact on jobs in the manufactural factor is by and large neutral.[22] Sectors such as hotel, catering,

---

20   Terry Gregory, Anna Salomons, and Ulrich Zierahn, "Racing with or against the Machine? Evidence from Europe," ZEW Discussion Paper 16–53, (Mannheim: Center for European Economic Research, 2016).

21   McKinsey Global Institute, Future That Works: Automation, Employment and Productivity (January 2017).

22   A survey of smart manufacturers by our research group in the Pearl River Delta region of China in August 2019 also reveals that AI and related technologies have not destroyed jobs in the manufacturing sector. The frontline manufacturing workers replaced by robots and smart devices are transferred to human-machine-collaboration jobs after being trained by their employers. Currently, Chinese smart manufacturers have not laid off low-skilled workers due to the use of robots and AI technologies. The reason is that, while reducing repetitive jobs, smart manufacturing increases maintenance, debugging

consumer services, manufacturing, and agricultural sectors account for a significant portion of China's economy. A large number of tasks in these sectors are repetitive and automatable. Therefore, worker displacement by AI-based automation in repetitive tasks in these sectors will lead to productivity improvement. As the economy continues to grow, AI technologies will create new products and services and lead to new jobs. Just as the Internet economy has, out of people's expectations, generated new jobs, AI will bring about similar changes in jobs. The productivity unleashed by AI and specialization in division of labor will provide new job opportunities.

Based on data from the CEES from 2015 to 2018, the effects of robots and smart devices on jobs in the manufacturing sector are estimated using a normative empirical research method.[23] The estimation results show that the use of robots and AI had a significant displacement effect on frontline manufacturing workers in China's manufacturing sector. The demand for such workers in enterprises using industrial robots and smart machines dropped by 19.6 percent, but the demand for middle- and top-level managers, R&D personnel, executives and clerks increased by 3.4 percent, 6.6 percent and 6.8 percent respectively. Assuming that frontline manufacturing workers in China are mainly migrant workers, it can be deduced that robots and AI may lead to a loss of about two million manufacturing jobs. It should be noted that the increase in percentage of the demand for middle- and top-level managers, R&D personnel, executives and clerks is not obtained by simply adding the share of each, because the base number and sample size of each occupation are different. The results of the quantitative research prove that the use of AI leads to new jobs and tasks in addition to improving productivity and output. Likewise, the decrease in the demand for frontline manufacturing workers is not the result of mass layoff. Instead, it shows a comparison with previous situation in terms of labor input when production is expanded for improvement in productivity and output.

The asymmetry between complex technological innovation and simple operation in work also puts workers, especially simple labor, in a disadvantageous negotiating position in the distribution of factor returns. The biggest challenge for China's human capital accumulation system is the gap between

---

and switching tasks and jobs such as automation engineers, automation technicians, inspection professionals, and smart production data analysts. In addition, the development of new technologies has made it easier for workers to acquire the operation skills of human-machine collaboration.

23   Albert Park, Qian Xuechao, and Qu Xiaobo, "The Effects of Robotics and Automation on Wage Inequality and Employment: Evidence from the China Employer-Employee Survey", (working paper, 2019).

the new demand for skills and job tasks and worker's skills as well as the difference in returns to skills. Compared with the impact of technologies on jobs, it is relatively easier to estimate the effects of technologies on demand for skills and returns to skills. In the long run, AI has the most significant impact on prices, because labor-cost-saving technologies allow firms to manufacture the same products at a lower cost. The consequent income effects may raise average income. In income distribution, however, there will be a further concentration of income among workers with skills preferred in the new technological revolution, which may widen the income gap between different groups of workers. The effects of robots and AI on the wages of groups with different skills in China's labor market are also estimated based on the CEES data. First, we examined the effects of robots and AI on the wages of groups of different human capital levels. The use of robots and AI will enable the group of workers with a higher level of human capital, i.e., people who have at least received junior college education, to earn significantly higher wages than other groups. With the average wages of middle- and top-level managers as a reference, on average, the impact of the use of robots or CNC (computer numerical control) machines and the value of robots and CNC machines is greater on wage premiums of workers with junior college and above education than on more experienced workers. The reason is that many middle-level managers in charge of production in manufacturing firms are promoted from frontline workers. They have the necessary skills, and they are capable of production process management, but their educational attainments are not necessarily better than other workers such as R&D personnel. Nonetheless, this reveals a very interesting point. It showcases that wage premiums resulting from technological innovation and use of new technologies are not only skill biased, but may also be knowledge biased. That means, general workers with a certain level of knowledge may enjoy such wage premiums. Second, we examined the effects of robots and smart devices on wages of jobs with different cognitive requirements. Jobs with high cognitive requirements gain a significantly higher technology premium than those with the other two types of cognitive requirements. In essence, it shows that skill-biased technological advancement results in higher wage premiums for jobs with higher cognitive requirements. It is worth noting that there is some fluctuation in the estimation results of robot's value, i.e., the impact of the share of robot's value in the value of firm's machines on wages for jobs with different cognitive requirements. The results are roughly the same for jobs with high and basic cognitive requirements, which may be attributable to the differences in distribution of the number and value of robots and the size of firm's assets. Third, we examined the impact of robots and smart devices on the wages of different professions and jobs. Significant differences are observed in the distribution of wage premiums generated by robots and AI technologies across professions and jobs. In other words, wage premiums resulting from productivity improvement following the adoption of new technologies are not equally available to all workers. Professions and jobs with higher skill requirements and higher levels of human capital receive higher wage premiums. Skill premiums resulting from the adoption of new technologies have reinforced the widening trend of the wage gap between skills and jobs.

While the new technological revolution can create lots of new jobs in China by raising productivity, the full impact of new technologies on China's labor market is yet to come. It is bound to be more far-reaching. In view of the great uncertainty about its impact on employment, the government should reconsider its policies for job creation. In addition, the government should pay great attention to vulnerable groups, and provide retraining programs for the unemployed and a stronger social security system for those having difficulty adapting to the new technological revolution.

4   Changes in Jobs and Trends of Job Tasks in China

In the new technological revolution, what are the jobs that are decreasing, increasing and disappearing in China's labor market? What new jobs are created? The new round of automation driven by the extensive use of robots and AI mainly affects routine and low-skilled job tasks. AI increases the automation of non-routine cognitive tasks previously performed by high-skilled workers. The changes in job tasks have led to a decreasing demand for skills that can be replaced by technologies, so, the changes in tasks reflect in essence the changes in demand for skills. What jobs will be replaced by automation and AI technologies? What skills will not be replaced by new technologies? The demand for high-level cognitive skills, social behavior skills and a combination of skills associated with greater adaptability is increasing. This trend is also observed in other developing countries. From 2000 to 2014, the proportion of employment in high-skilled occupations rose by eight percentage points in Bolivia and thirteen percentage points in Ethiopia. The changes in employment show up not only through new jobs replacing old ones, but also through the changing skill requirements of existing jobs.[24]

---

24   World Bank, *World Development Report 2019: The Changing Nature of Work* (World Bank Group, 2019).

Data from China's population censuses in 1990, 2000, 2005, 2010 and 2015 can reflect the changes, characteristics and trends of the employment structure in China in the context of the new technological revolution. Cortes et al. (2016) and Du et al. (2018) divide the jobs of the working-age population into routine and non-routine ones according to their automatability and possibility of being replaced by computers. Routine and non-routine jobs are subdivided into manual and cognitive jobs according to their skill requirements. Routine manual (RM) stands for manual jobs that can be easily replaced by automation-biased technologies such as computers, robots, AI and so on, including assembly line workers. Non-routine manual (NRM) stands for uncodifiable jobs that cannot be easily replaced by automation-biased technologies, such as food preparation and serving jobs. Routine cognitive (RC) stands for cognitive jobs that can be easily replaced by automation-biased technologies, such as computing, repetitive customer service and so on. Non-routine cognitive (NRC) stands for cognitive jobs that are highly complementary to automation-biased technologies, such as executives, technicians and so on.

Figure 7.2 shows the changes with regard to NRC, NRM, RC and RM in China based on population censuses from 1990 to 2015. Overall the trends of job changes in China over the past decades are consistent with technological progress and the adoption of new technologies. Non-routine tasks have been growing significantly, while routine tasks show a clear downward trend despite fluctuations in the context of economic growth and output expansion. Such changes demonstrate that new technologies reduce repetitive and codifiable routine tasks, which is consistent with the experience of other countries and a common phenomenon. In addition, the distribution of the shares of RC tasks in the years concerned is a good illustration that new technologies increase the demand for tasks biased in favor of both technologies and knowledge. Therefore, the job changes in China are similar to the changes revealed by the World Bank in terms of the nature of jobs and demand for skills.[25] New technologies lead to an increase in the demand for non-repetitive cognitive skills, communication skills and social behavior skills.

Based on the population census data, we also identified the increasing and decreasing occupations in China from 1990 to 2015, thereby examining and analyzing the changes in the employment structure in China's labor market. Table 7.1 shows the following changes. First, the share of warehouse workers, construction workers, construction technicians, agricultural and

---

25   World Bank, *World Development Report 2019: The Changing Nature of Work* (World Bank Group, 2019).

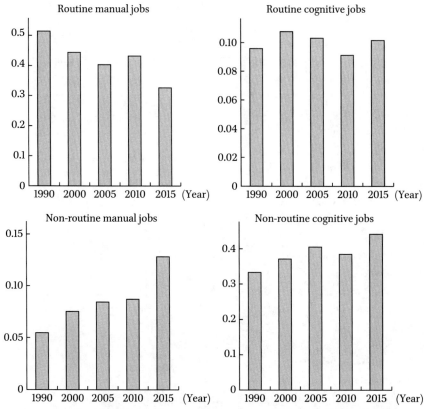

FIGURE 7.2   Changes in employment structure and job tasks in China from 1990 to 2015

forestry technicians, and airplane and ship technicians was increasing. Second, the share of miscellaneous commercial and service workers, literature, art and sports workers, legal professionals and scientific researchers was also increasing. This not only reflects a greater demand for skill-biased jobs arising from the use of new technologies, but also shows that new technologies have been creating new jobs and tasks. Third, the share of some jobs is decreasing, including miscellaneous operators of manufacturing and transport facilities, other manufacturing workers and related workers, wood processing and wood-based panel manufacturing workers, plastic and rubber products manufacturing workers, workers producing and processing grain and oil, food and beverages, and fodder, and leather products makers. The decline mirrors a decreasing demand for skills required for repetitive tasks. Moreover, as the official categorization of occupations and alteration to the names of occupations lag behind the practical economic situation in China, many new occupations are not included in the list of occupations in population census.

TABLE 7.1   Changes in China's occupational shares from 1990 to 2015 based on population
census data

Occupation	Type	1990	2000	2005	2010	2015	Change from 1990 to 2015
Warehousing workers	NRM	0.77	2.85	3.39	3.31	7.27	+
Head of firms and other establishments	NRC	3.85	3.31	2.85	2.92	2.75	−
Head of Party and mass organizations	NRC	1.39	0.73	0.46	0.23	0.01	−
Miscellaneous technicians	NRM	0.11	0.09	0.24	0.14	0.81	+
Miscellaneous clerks and related workers	RC	0.27	0.53	0.97	0.67	0.26	−
Miscellaneous commercial and service workers	NRC	0.66	4.97	6.61	6.2	9.18	+
Miscellaneous operators of manufacturing and transportation facilities	RM	6.48	3.67	8.32	3.55	0.22	−
Miscellaneous manufacturing workers and related workers	RM	11.99	10.77	4.97	10.55	5.79	−
Surveyors and mine workers	RM	2.39	1.63	1.5	1.22	0.96	−
Chemical producers	RM	0.98	0.84	0.87	0.79	0.81	−
Healthcare professionals	NRC	2.41	2.43	2.29	1.84	2.09	−
Printing workers	RM	0.61	0.44	0.39	0.31	0.24	−
Head of state departments and related agencies	NRC	0.71	0.66	0.35	0.29	0.19	−
Security workers and firefighters	NRM	2.15	2.26	2.14	2.27	1.5	−
Construction technicians, agricultural and forestry technicians	NRM	2.37	2.29	2.65	2.99	3.22	+
Construction workers	RM	4.05	5.26	5.65	7.88	9.79	+
Teachers	NRC	5.91	5.59	4.48	3.92	3.91	−
Literature, art and sports workers	NRC	0.25	0.21	0.28	0.3	0.57	+

TABLE 7.1   Changes in China's occupational shares from 1990 to 2015 (*cont.*)

Occupation	Type	1990	2000	2005	2010	2015	Change from 1990 to 2015
Press and publication workers, cultural workers	NRC	0.55	0.41	0.3	0.3	0.19	–
Wood processing and wood-based panel manufacturing workers	RM	3.15	2.36	1.77	1.95	1.53	–
Checkers, weighers, measurers	RM	1.95	1.39	0.99	1.04	2.66	+
Rubber and plastic products manufacturing workers	RM	0.79	0.71	0.87	0.74	0.62	–
Legal professionals	NRC	0.19	0.21	0.19	0.17	0.28	+
Tobacco and tobacco products processing workers	RM	0.08	0.06	0.05	0.05	0.05	–
Manufacturing workers making glass, porcelain and products made from glass and porcelain	RM	0.51	0.5	0.51	0.49	1.09	+
Power equipment installers, operators, and repairers, power supply workers	RM	2.95	1.92	1.42	1.32	1.83	–
Scientific researchers	NRC	0.1	0.12	3.55	0.13	0.12	+
Workers producing and processing grain and oil, food and beverages, and fodder	RM	1.75	1.71	1.37	1.11	1.36	–
Fabricating, knitting, and printing and dyeing workers	RM	3.67	2.35	2.02	1.78	0.95	–
Brokers	RC	6.23	4.77	3.76	3.47	3.76	–
Office and administrative workers	RC	3.08	5.46	5.64	5.01	6.1	+
Tailors, leather workers	RM	3.22	3.93	3.69	4.85	3.47	+

TABLE 7.1   Changes in China's occupational shares from 1990 to 2015 (*cont.*)

Occupation	Type	1990	2000	2005	2010	2015	Change from 1990 to 2015
Salespeople	NRC	9.86	15.07	15.31	18.33	19.14	+
Transport facility operators and related workers	RM	5.43	6.18	5.3	5	0.76	–
Metal smelting workers, sheet metal workers	RM	1.52	0.79	0.93	0.89	0.78	–
Airplane and ship technicians	NRM	0.07	0.05	0.03	0.04	0.02	–
Food preparation and serving workers	NRC	7.55	3.47	3.9	3.96	5.72	–

Note: RM stands for routine manual jobs. RC stands for routine cognitive jobs. NRM stands for non-routine manual jobs. NRC stands for non-routine cognitive jobs.
SOURCE: CALCULATION BASED ON MICRO DATA FROM CHINA'S POPULATION CENSUSES IN 1990, 2000 AND 2010 AND ONE-PERCENT NATIONAL POPULATION SAMPLE SURVEYS IN 2005 AND 2015

5   China's Policy Responses to the Changes Arising from the New Technological Revolution

Currently, China's demographic dividend as an economic growth driver is rapidly waning. In addition, the narrowing technology gap between economies will lead to diminishing latecomer advantages. China needs to seize the opportunities for development thanks to the new technological revolution and proactively respond to the challenges of new technologies such as robots and AI. It will significantly facilitate China's shift from high-speed development to high-quality development, and help China to pursue development relying on AI. If measures are taken on various fronts such as policies, institutions and public awareness to expedite the transition towards an innovation-driven economy, China can also use AI to bolster its weaknesses in economic and social development.

Technological advancement will lead to major and unpredictable changes. The appearance of new jobs and occupations reflects the extensive adoption and development of new technologies in China. The technological innovation and rapid adoption of AI in China are having an impact on the global technology market, and technologies such as digital technologies, mobile payment and sharing economy are spreading across the world as China opens wider. Such development and advantages of China are inseparable from the government's innovation-driven development strategy, policy support and deepening reform. The pattern of technological advancement and development in which the government plays a leading role is worth promoting and exploring. In making policies on industries, technological innovation, and adoption of technologies, the government should adopt a long-term perspective, support and guide enterprises in technological transformation and upgrading. Policies supporting technological innovation should highlight the role of enterprises in research and development for technological transformation and adoption, and provide support to original research and development in terms of funding, research and talents. Measures should be taken to help and encourage enterprises to establish laboratories transformed and upgraded with AI, and encourage them to cultivate and tap into the full potential of employees. Policies promoting the use of AI technologies should cater to the needs of enterprises in automation and adoption of smart technologies. The limited financial support from the government should be used to promote machine learning, algorithms, AI application and so on.

Policy responses and forecasts should be made with a big-picture thinking and consider measures to avoid the negative impact of robots and AI. In big cities such as Beijing, Shanghai, Guangzhou and Shenzhen, primary and middle school students spend much time each year learning about robots and model aircrafts, and even attend national robot competitions, so they have hands-on experience of AI, robots and 3D printing. In poor areas, however, children may have never seen a computer in their life, and have no idea about the progress of our time. Considering the situation, precautionary policies are required to prepare the whole society, especially those in the education and vocational training sectors, for the new technological revolution, so that the labor force and talent structure can adapt to the changes coming with AI. Efforts should also be intensified to improve data and AI literacy in the labor force of all age groups. Policymakers should make constant efforts in education in relevant fields to ensure that the future labor force are equipped with necessary skills to adapt to technological advancement. In addition to building talent pools of data scientists and engineers, efforts are required to inform the majority of the labor force of how new technologies are used in different fields and industries. Schools should place greater emphasis on science, technology, engineering, mathematics and similar subjects. Basic education and vocational training should also include data science courses.

In response to the new technological revolution, the education and training sectors should focus on skills essential for future jobs and tasks. As AI technologies and other new technologies are spreading fast and applied in a wide range of fields, the labor force will find a mismatch between their knowledge acquired at university and the advancing technology. In the context of the new technological revolution, the education and training sectors should cater to a dynamic labor market that values skills over degrees. In investment in human resources, in addition to basic skills, it is important to improve their advanced cognitive skills and social behavior skills, for which investment in early childhood education is required. Human capital is vital to addressing the negative impacts of automation. A lasting challenge for future employment efforts is to help the workers hit by AI to readjust and acquire new skills. Employment authorities must identify jobs that are most likely to be replaced by automation and retrain the affected workers. They can, for example, arrange for vocational schools and enterprises and other private organizations to provide free education for workers.

China needs to improve the existing social security system, expand social insurance coverage and create a social insurance system that rebalances labor, capital and technology. In view of the changes in job tasks and the nature of job brought about by robots and AI, social insurance and social protection systems should be adjusted to create a fairer and sustainable social security system. While robots and AI will not have a severe impact on the jobs of the existing labor force in manufacturing enterprises in the short term, they have surely reduced the long-term demand for low-skilled workers. The extensive use of AI will also have a significant negative impact on the wage growth of low-skilled workers. The social security system based on primarily payroll taxes and directly connected with employment will thus face new challenges. Due to unemployment and income disparity caused by AI technologies, the number of dependents will increase, and the contribution base of workers may decrease, resulting in increased pressure on the social security system in terms of both financing and payment. The social security system should consider a shift from humans to capital as financing sources. For example, robot taxes can be introduced to compensate workers. Institution design efforts in this regard shall be started as soon as possible to study its conditions and implementation.

Bibliography

Acemoglu, Daron, and Pascual Restrepo. "Robots and Jobs: Evidence from US Labor Markets." In *Working Paper 23285*. National Bureau of Economic Research, 2017.

Acemoglu, Daron, and Pascual Restrepo. "The Race between Machine and Man: Implications of Technology for Growth, Factor Shares and Employment." *American Economic Review* 108, no. 6 (2018): 1488–1542.

Agrawal, Ajay, John McHale, and Alex Oettl, *Artificial Intelligence and Recombinant Growth*. Toronto: University of Toronto, 2017.

Du, Yang, Jia Peng, and Cheng Jie. "Structural Changes in Labor Market, Job Tasks and Skill Demand." *Studies in Labor Economics*, no. 3 (2017).

Elsby, Michael W.L., Bart Hobijn, and Aysegul Sahin. "The Decline of the U.S. Labor Share." *Brookings Papers on Economic Activity*, no. 2 (2013): 1–63.

Graetz, Georg, and Guy Michaels. *Robots at Work*. London: London School of Economics, 2018.

James, Bessen. *Learning by Doing: The Real Connection between Innovation, Wages, and Wealth*. New Haven: Yale University Press, 2016.

Jorgenson, Dale W., Mun S. Ho, and Jon D. Samuels. *Educational Attainment and the Revival of U.S. Economic Growth*. Chicago: University of Chicago Press, 2017.

Index

Printed in the United States
by Baker & Taylor Publisher Services